THE ART OF WRITING LITERATURE ESSAYS

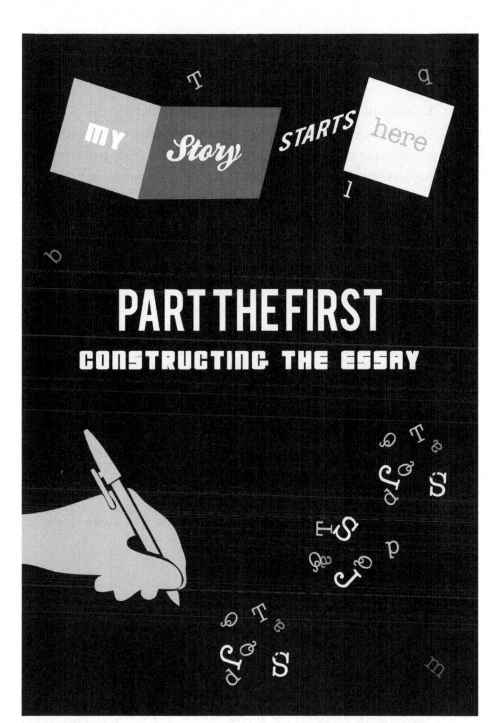

MY Story STARTS here

PART THE FIRST
CONSTRUCTING THE ESSAY

PART THE FIRST: Constructing the Essay

1. Introduction: Key Features of Successful Essays

The fundamental questions about any work of literature focus on just two aspects: what the text has to say and how it says it. First and foremost, a successful literature essay articulates a well considered response to the ideas developed in a text and to the techniques used within it.

What are the other key features of good A-level literature essays? Have a go at listing them now, before reading on. Once you've listed these features try putting them in order of importance. Then compare your list with ours.

We think that a good literature essay:

1. answers the question
2. is well-structured, developing a clear line of argument
3. uses textual evidence effectively
4. includes close analysis of language
5. is well expressed and accurately written
6. uses a range of contexts effectively
7. is interesting for the reader
8. has a strong introduction and conclusion
9. demonstrates independent thought, personal engagement and some originality
10. engages in informed critical debate
11. uses an advanced critical vocabulary
12. fulfils the assessment objectives

Of course, all of these are potentially valuable features and you may be able to come up with a few more. Which of these is the most and least important varies depending on what sort of literary essay you're writing, what sort of question you're answering and in what context. Essentially, however, in this book we will argue that the best A-level literature essays express the **critical**

thoughts of a student, informed and refined by other readers, in the voice of that student. In other words, we do not consider a simple repackaging of material from a revision guide, or the repetition of information delivered by a teacher, however fluent, to constitute successful literature essay writing.

Perhaps, a more pertinent question than 'what makes a good A-level literature essay?" is 'what is an essay?' We are very familiar with the noun 'essay', the written piece you submit. But if you consider the verb 'essay' (what you are actually doing when constructing your essay) you will see that you are involved in an intellectual 'attempt' or 'testing' or 'trialling'. But what is it you are attempting / trying / testing / trialling? These keywords capture the essential difference between writing literature essays at GCSE and at A-level.

At A-level, essays operate on several different levels. Essentially, they are functional in that they serve to prepare you for your exams or they fulfil your coursework requirements. However, on a more fundamental level they crystallise your thoughts about a certain aspect of a literary text. Your brain will be crammed with conflicting information, all of varying quality, you have received from your teachers, your classmates, critics you've read etc. But how do you find out what *you* think? This essentially is what you are attempting / trying / testing / trialling. While you are attempting to answer the question you have been given, more importantly, you are simultaneously discovering and developing your own critical voice.

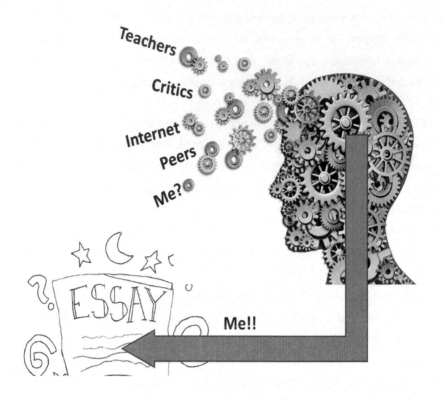

At A-level, your essays should filter out what you don't subscribe to; ultimately, it condenses the many competing voices in your head until it becomes one: your own. You will find that the more essays you write about a text or author, the more confident you become in thinking and speaking about that text or author. In most cases, it is not what you read, but **what you write after you read** that paves the way to detailed literary understanding. In fact, you will probably start to interrogate and re-examine what you've previously written as you develop as a literature student. Such a self-reflective approach is a key sign of the outstanding literature student. This is what makes essay writing such an essential activity in literary study: it is a record of your own self-development.

Ideas and Opinions
As an academic subject, English Literature does not deal in absolute knowledge; rather it is about informed **opinions and ideas, values and**

feelings. The experience of studying English at A-level will be rewarding if you are prepared to think for yourself, to consider and critique what other people have thought and said, and to express in your own voice your critical opinions as cogently and lucidly as you are able. That is what this book will attempt to help you to do.

We advise you to be suspicious of books, websites or teachers (!) offering a one-size-fits-all, foolproof, off-the-shelf approach to literary texts and to writing literary essays. Scaffolding, like modelling, is useful, especially early in your course. But scaffolding can become rigid and restrictive, a straightjacket forcing your essay into a preset shape. Think of scaffolding as the equivalent of arm-bands and floats for swimmers. Helpful at first, these aids have to be taken away for you to swim properly and independently.

So, the bad news is...whatever some websites might claim, **there's no single secret formula, guide, model or programme for a good A-level literature essay**. Writing an essay is not like constructing a piece of IKEA furniture (thankfully) or an Airfix model (luckily). There's no set pattern you have to follow rigidly and unthinkingly. But the good news is...there's no set pattern you have to follow rigidly. This means that in writing your essays you have the freedom to express yourself. This doesn't indicate, however, that you can luxuriate in an anarchy of interpretation, that anything goes or that you can simply say anything you like in whatever way you choose. Not, at least, if you hope to achieve a high grade. There are, of course, academic conventions within which you have freedom. And, of course, some structure is helpful, just as the complete lack of structure would be debilitating.

As you should know, examination boards also set out assessment objectives which provide further guidance for your response. Assessment objectives also reveal the values and ideas about literary study and writing about literature underpinning all A-level English Literature courses. So, they're worth our attention. **A student who pays no attention to assessment objectives and the arcana of their weighting on particular modules is unlikely to reach the top grades.** The trick is to write essays with the assessment objectives in mind without writing merely to hit them like targets or jump through them like hoops.

Learning how to structure essays effectively should be part of your English Literature A-level course. Use an 'off-the-shelf' essay formula and you deny yourself the chance to structure your essay in a way that you see as most fit to the effective expression of the ideas you want to explore and the argument you wish to articulate.

A golden formula?

Back in the dark ages, one of our English Literature A-level teachers supplied a gold-plated, foolproof formula to ensure we scored high grades in our practical criticism paper. Practical criticism is a term referring to the analysis of previously unseen texts presented without any contextualising information. This golden formula was very memorable, as proven by the fact that we can still remember it today:

TOC KF VPIF MRS EAR

T = theme, O= organisation of ideas, C= context, KF = kinds of feelings (a rather vague one this), V = verse form, P = personification, I = can't remember this one (imagery, perhaps), F= figures of speech, M = metre, R = rhythm, S = stanza form, E = enjambment, A = alliteration and R = rhyme.

Obviously this formula was intended as a handy checklist of the sorts of things to write about on a poem. It was also intended as a blueprint for an essay, so that TOC indicated what material we should cover in the introduction. Think about it for a moment, though, and the blueprint seems pretty random. Why, for instance, should personification be lumped with verse form? In fact, different aspects of poems are rather unhelpfully thrown together: linguistic features, such as imagery, formal features, such as stanza form and sonic aspects, such as alliteration, are placed in a rather haphazard pile.

Though the checklist was well meaning, used as a blueprint it imposed a virtually random, predetermined structure on practical criticism essays. Why, we might ask (trying hard not to sound smug and supercilious) is context only ever referred to in the introduction? And isn't writing about the ideas in a text fundamental to the whole essay and therefore not something that can just be ticked off at the start? In our (bitter and painful) experience, not all teachers welcome this sort of questioning. But to be a really good English Literature student you really must develop a critical attitude, including towards what teachers and critics tell you.

Such set formulas are, then, limited and limiting. You will probably be familiar with the PEA or PEE formula from GCSE for constructing analytical paragraphs. You may also have been told to use discourse markers, those little words that signpost the direction of your essay, such as 'firstly', secondly', 'in comparison' or 'moreover'. While PEA and discourse markers are useful as guides, over-reliance on them makes essays feel clunkily mechanical. An ex-student of ours, reading English at Oxford, was told in her first year to purge her essays of the discourse markers she routinely used at the start of each of her paragraphs. (Advice that echoed our own!)

Preferences for particular essay structures are partly cultural. In some cultures it is considered inelegant, for instance, to begin an essay with a thesis statement and from there to go on to test this line of argument against the hard evidence of textual detail. Such an approach is considered too linear. Instead, it is thought better that the thesis is worked towards during the essay. However, **starting with a thesis, argument or hypothesis** and then examining the data in the body of the essay before arriving at a conclusion at the end is the dominant essay model in the Western cultural tradition. It is also the structure most favoured by examination boards. So, more or less, it will be the model we will recommend in this book.

Essay Structure

The structure of your essay can be distilled down into the following simplistic description.

introduction: outline of the argument / thesis and overview of the issues
main body: examination of the argument / thesis through exploration of textual material
conclusion: evaluation and potential modification of thesis

Although simplistic it is worth keeping it in mind as you begin your essay planning. The most important point to bear in mind is that you need a clear argument articulated succinctly in your introduction and that the rest of your discussion must explore this argument. If your discussion does not contribute to your central argument then you must jettison it into the container marked 'sounds great but not actually useful'!

Sometimes students worry if new ideas emerge in writing their essay which take them in a new direction or which do not fit with their thesis. Good essays are exploratory - **writing is a form of thinking and thinking is always dynamic and in flux**. Adapting your plan and shifting your argument in the light of new findings is a sign of strength and flexible thinking rather than of weakness, as long as you show awareness of these shifts in your thinking. A conclusion that significantly modifies the thesis set out in the introduction will almost always be an effective one, as long as you acknowledge that your argument has developed. It cannot be a case of you realising you've arrived at a very different destination and just hoping nobody will notice...like an unreliable tourist guide.

Horror Writing [and not the good variety...]

Studying disease is a helpful method for understanding health. By analogy examining diseased essays can help us more easily identify what health might entail. (If you're a bit squeamish you may want to read these pox-ridden shockers pretty swiftly). They are both introductory paragraphs, the first is a response to a question about the presentation of old age in the poem *Sailing to Byzantium* by W. B. Yeats; the second is on *Frankenstein* by Mary Shelley:

1. In this essay I am going to write about the presentation of age in Yeats' wonderful poem 'S2B'. Yeats writes brilliantly about age in this amazing poem, which he wrote when he himself was getting pretty old (over fifty). In the time in which it was written he was also really unhappy because Ireland (where he lived) was struggling with its separation from England. Yeats was Anglo-Irish, not a Catholic, too. Yeats uses language in the poem as well as the form and structure to convey his various views of age, as well as of nature, art and the place 'Byzantium', all of which I will be writing about in this essay. The tone of the poem is really depressing and sad and what the poet is trying to say is that he doesn't want to die.

2. frankenstein by mary shelley written in the victorian period (1918) was a book about transgression in lots of ways which in this essay I am going to explore through its presentation which is a key aspect of what david bottling defines as the gothic. the gothic was a type of literature that started ages ago with a book called the castle of othello and featured evil villains and virtuous heroines which were chased around castles in faraway places which shelley transgresses herself because she makes her male character the protagonist who is both chased and chased by the monster he creates which is because shelly was writing at the end of the first blossoming of gothic literature in 1762. Which also shows that in some ways the binary oppositions which underpin our understanding of the world, such as up/down, good/bad,

hero/villain and the ultimate one alive/dead are as andrew Green says 'problematised' by the gothic, as the monster can be seen as a double for 'Frankenstein' from what is known as a psychological viewpoint. The ways in which the book shows transgression is through it's characters, narration, language and action.

Okay, that's more than enough of that. So what's wrong with these sickly specimens? Before reading ahead, have a go at listing their faults. Don't worry, no students were hurt in the making of these introductions - they were written by a teacher to demonstrate how not to write - so you can be as brutal as you like!

Essay 1
- The opening sentence establishes a naive style and merely repeats the information in the question. Therefore, it is waffle and worth zero marks. Cut to the chase!
- Using empty words of praise such as 'amazing', 'wonderful' and 'brilliantly' is not critical evaluation. Without evidence, such comments are worth zip.
- 'In the time it was written...' this is a phrase that crops up far too often in essays. How is the examiner to know that the candidate knows the socio-historical context and its impact on the text? The golden rule is to be specific. If it's a late Victorian or early twentieth century poem say so.
- The link between the poet's aging and the context is implicit at best; 'really unhappy' is not a very precise description of Yeats's complex feelings about Ireland.
- The point about his Anglo-Irishness is dumped into the essay and undeveloped; it could have opened up a revealing line of critical enquiry.
- There is no link to the following sentence about the poem's language.
- What writer doesn't use words? Again this sort of windy, generalised comment is worth no marks. Marks would be awarded if the candidate established what sort of language the poet used and how he employed

this to dramatise his ideas.

- 'His various views about age...' So what are these? Be specific, for crying out loud!
- There is no link to the point about tone.
- 'what the poet is trying to say' implies that the candidate is more articulate than the poet and has a better idea of what the latter is trying, rather ineffectually to express. A bold and rather foolish assumption.
- 'he doesn't want to die' is perhaps an oversimplification of Yeats's views about old age.

No doubt you will be able to find more errors, problems and weaknesses. What should be clear is that, although the student does know something about the text and about how to respond effectively to the question, they haven't learnt to express this effectively in an essay.

We'll leave the *Frankenstein* essay introduction to fester for now. If you can't wait to diagnose what's wrong with it, and this introduction is at death's door, let nature take its course and let it die without dignity.

So what does a healthy essay look like? Read the following introduction and try to identify the various ways in which this one is better than the previous two. This essay discusses the theme of transformation in *The Second Coming*, also by W.B.Yeats.

Published in Yeats' 1927 collection, 'Michael Robartes and the Dancer', 'The Second Coming' dwells on the violent nature of radical change. As he does in other poems in this selection, such as 'Easter 1916' and 'Leda and the Swan', Yeats presents this violence ambivalently. On the one hand, he is terrified by the potentially destructive forces unleashed as things spin out of control; on the other he seems exhilarated and awestruck by the energy and drama. By the time he wrote 'The Second Coming' the violence in Ireland, and indeed, on the world stage had grown to the point where Yeats' vision of the future became a vision of an apocalypse.

Isn't that so much better? Of course it is. The writing's clear, well focused and cogent. We feel we can trust this writer; that they know what they're talking about and are skilful in expressing this.

In the next section we'll take some of the essential characteristics of good essays we listed earlier and examine each of them in a little more detail. We'll start with 'answering the question' and finish part one of this book with some advice on plagiarism and referencing.

2. Understanding and Answering the Question

Questions set on A-level English Literature papers fall into types, each type focusing on a specific aspect of the text, or texts, studied. The most frequently asked questions centre on the first three aspects in the following list:

1. Character
2. Character relationships
3. Themes
4. Genre
5. Language
6. Structure

We'll examine how you should set about answering each of these types of questions in the sections on writing about particular types of texts. Our interest here is more on the sorts of questions you'll be asked in essays. Often examination boards use a small, select group of verbs in their essay questions:

'discuss'   'explore'   'explain'   'examine'

To this list can be added phrases such as **'to what extent do you agree...'** and **'Evaluate the view that...'** which are often tagged to a critical quotation or statement about a text. What exactly do these imperative verbs indicate about the nature of the task you face? In what ways, for instance, is the instruction to 'discuss how Wilfred Owen conveys the experience of comradeship in *Strange Meeting'* different from the question 'how does Wilfred Owen convey the experience of comradeship in *Strange Meeting'* or 'what are the experiences of comradeship articulated in *Strange Meeting*?'

Discussion implies that the issues at hand have not been resolved absolutely one way or another. It suggests that different people may take different views on these issues - a discussion of a single view would be rather limited. In other words, the texts are fundamentally open; open for, and to, debate. A discussion might also include a critical evaluation of the ideas themselves and of how successfully they are communicated in the text.

Notice too the importance of that small, easily missable word '**how**'. What does this word imply? Sometimes examination boards use the phrase 'explore the presentation of...' This has the same function as 'how', signalling you to focus on the techniques the writer uses to present their ideas.

It is almost universally the case that the better the student the closer the attention they will pay to the nuances of language. This means the language of the text they are studying, but also the language of the question they are answering. At A2 and degree level, the latter becomes more significant as the questions grow more complex and more subtly worded. Weaker students generally ignore the 'discuss' instruction as well as the 'how' / 'presentation of...' part of the question. Instead they will hone in on the most familiar words and write about those. In the Wilfred Owen example this might lead to a listing of examples of comradeship in the poem *Strange Meeting*.

Often these students haven't fully grasped that English Literature essays are not simply vehicles for the repeating of remembered, incontestable facts. They haven't fully understood that meaning in literature is always conditional and therefore the subject of debate, bias, opinion, argument, enlightenment and originality. These are things that make the best writing about literature so vibrant and alive.

For example, one student might admire how a poet like Wordsworth adapts the conventions of pastoral literature in his poems. The student might point to his relocating of the pastoral in wild, uncultivated landscapes and his use of plain, ordinary everyday language as admirable qualities. Another student, however, might argue that Wordsworth's masculine gaze objectives, passifies and feminises nature in a way that is entirely conventional and arguably degrading to women. We hope you'll agree it is the debate about ideas, technique and aesthetics that makes the subject most interesting.

In a really good essay a student will be alert to the implications of the wording of the question and will explore the different techniques the writer uses, considering how these contribute to the text's themes or concerns. This superior student will also situate their critical opinion within critical debate about the text by other readers, using the other readings as a tool for testing and honing their own critical ideas.

If the writer of the text is a poet, these techniques might include figurative and sensory imagery, sonic effects, such as assonance or onomatopoeia, and structural devices such as metre or stanzas. The superior student will also consider what the writer actually has to say about comradeship and will notice and explore the angle the writer has taken on his or her subject.

'**Explore**' and '**examine**' similarly suggest an open process of investigation whose results are to be determined in the essay. An exploration, or examination, requires a careful, close and alert inspection of the textual terrain.

Phrases such as '**evaluate the view** that...' and '**to what extent** do you agree...' signal that there is more than one opinion about the issue at hand. These phrases imply that you may not entirely agree with the critical position stated in the question. We will explore how you can write about different interpretations later when we look at responses to specific types of texts. But, for now, what's clear is that these phrases encourage us to consider arguments in favour of a proposition, but also to be alert to possible counter arguments. The ability to mount effective counter arguments is another important indicator differentiating between levels of response.

Essay Questions Hoisted on to the Dissecting Table

Okay, we'll try to apply all this to a sample question. Imagine you are set the question 'To what extent do you agree that Lear's psychological flaws cause the tragedy of *King Lear*?'

(Don't worry if you're not familiar with the play; it's the approach to a question that's important here.)

In our plan we'd jot down **some ideas to support this contention**. For example, he is the King in the play and he therefore wields power; the decision to split the kingdom and share it between his daughters is also Lear's; his vanity and moral blindness lead to his deception by his elder daughters and his banishment of his youngest, loyal daughter, Cordelia. As all these contribute to the tragedy it is reasonable to conclude that Lear is indeed responsible for the tragedy, at least to some extent.

But we would also **need to think of counter arguments**. For example, the culpability of other characters, such as the various elder sisters, the ruthless villain, Edmund, or the foolish courtier, Gloucester. Their actions definitely contribute to the tragic turn of events. Above and beyond character we could argue that tragedies are caused by ideas, by the clash of ideologies. Patriarchal values, perhaps monarchical values, contribute significantly to the tragedy. Perhaps too Shakespeare's plays dramatise the forces of history, embodied by characters. In this reading, the tragedy is caused by the traumatic birth of the early modern out of the medieval past; all the characters, including Lear, are victims of the steamroller of history.

We said that the best candidates pay closest attention to the language of the text and of the question set. This question, for example, identifies Lear's mind as the source of the tragedy - suggesting a psychoanalytical reading of the play. If we are to blame Lear most then, perhaps, we should point to his actions and words; as a fictional character he doesn't actually have a psyche, we could argue. In this way, **the best responses unpick the presuppositions of the questions (their unstated values and beliefs that underpin the critical approach).** This is a high level skill, one that you'll want to develop as you move through AS into A2 and beyond. We'll now have a quick go at practising it here.

Look closely at the following questions taken from various A-level English Literature exams on Shakespeare's plays. Try to identify the traps less successful essay responses might fall into in each question and how stronger responses would demonstrate alertness to the wording. As with the Lear question, the fact that you might not know these plays shouldn't prevent you from doing this exercise successfully:

1. By exploring the dramatic presentation of Orsino in *Twelfth Night*, evaluate the view that he is a 'romantic fantasist who urgently needs to be awakened to reality'.

2. 'The women in *Othello* are articulate, but frustratingly unable to save themselves from the cruelty of men'. Evaluate this view by exploring the presentation of women and their situations in the play.

3. 'The bitter and artificial world of the court needs the natural, pastoral world for its renewal.' By exploring these contrasting elements of *The Winter's Tale*, evaluate this view of the play.

4. The world of the Tavern is more dramatically significant than the world of the court.' Evaluate this view by exploring Shakespeare's use of contrasting settings in *Henry IV Part 1*.

For question 1, less successful responses will focus on the character Orsino. As he is a major character in *Twelfth Night* every student studying the play will have written notes and perhaps essays on him. The temptation to repeat notes may be hard to resist, but resist you must. The weakest responses will be character studies, treating him as if he is a real person, outlining what Orsino does and says and why we should or shouldn't like him.

Better responses will explore the **dramatic presentation** (through dialogue, soliloquy, through what other characters say about him, through his language and his actions, costume, props etc.). These responses will develop arguments as well as counter arguments to the proposition that he is a '**romantic fantasist**', interrogating the meaning of both those words. The best responses will also consider whether he does in fact need to be '**awakened to reality**' and whether there is any '**urgency**' in this matter. That's quite a lot of ground to cover.

For question 2, weaker responses will probably repeat pre-prepared essays on the women in *Othello*. The weakest will ignore 'the presentation of...' to write character studies, maybe with a few major female characters written about in a straightforward sequence.

Better responses will explore whether the women are presented as being '**articulate**', whether they really are '**unable to save themselves**', whether the effect of this on the audience is a feeling of frustration and, finally, whether the single cause of their suffering is the '**cruelty of men**'. Perhaps, for example, their suffering could be caused by the cruelty of other women, the love of men or those monumental, flattening forces of history we mentioned earlier...

In his introduction to the play *The History Boys*, Alan Bennett recalls learning the trick of answering questions at University in a way that avoided being obvious and pedestrian:

'I also twigged what somebody ought to have taught me but never had, namely that there was a journalistic side to answering an examination question; that going for the wrong end of the stick was more attention-grabbing than a less unconventional approach, however balanced...Once I'd got into the way of turning a question on its head in the way Irwin [one of the teachers in the play] describes I began to get pleasure out of the technique itself, sketching out skeleton answers to all sorts of questions and using the same facts, for instance, to argue opposite points of view...'

In other words, Bennett discovered that every question has a front door and a back door and that an answer that approaches by the back door is much more likely to interest your reader. **Be prepared, therefore, to try to take an unusual angle on a question, to avoid the obvious response**. Writing about a Shakespeare play you are joining a long line of previous writers. Though you need to show your awareness of the old ground, try to  open up some new terrain somewhere in your essay, or to provide a different perspective on the familiar literary landscape you're exploring.

Of course, your whole essay does not have to be original. That would be rather a tall order. Rather, ideally, you should **aim to try somewhere within your essay to deviate a little from conventional wisdom** or a conventional approach to a question. This space will allow you to express your own independent thinking and help distinguish your essay from the hundreds of others the examiners have to mark. We know from experience that examiners really appreciate coming across some new and original thinking. They tend also to reward it handsomely.

For example, on a Shakespeare play it is relatively uncommon to come across an examination of a central theme through the presentation of a very minor character. In Dr Emma Smith's excellent (and free) podcasts of her Oxford Shakespeare lectures, she explores *Twelfth Night* through the prism of the curiously silent presence of the minor character of the sea captain, Antonio, in the final scene of the play. This is a method that can easily be adopted and adapted: find a really minor character in the text, one that you know few people will notice or comment on, and examine the central issues of the text through their contribution.

In a similar way, the majority of students focus on imagery when writing about poems. Very few consider syntax, the order of words within a sentence. Yet such sentence structuring has a major impact on the effect of words. Really sophisticated analysis would explore the combined effect of imagery working with or against syntax in relation to a text's themes.

One final example of taking a slightly unusual angle on a question: writing on the dramatic impact of Iago in *Othello* one student wrote about how the experience of listening to an audio recording of the play affected her interpretation. As a disembodied voice Iago seemed more sinister and he was harder to empathise with, they argued. Here, the student cleverly used the context of their reception of the play to further their argument.

Consider the front door of a question. Imagine the back door, or the side door, or the window. Try to come at the question through one of those openings.

3. Developing a Clear Line of Argument

When planning your response to a question, start by jotting down the points you want to make. Try to turn the question around a bit, as suggested above, paying particular attention to key words and phrases. The next stage is to **order your points, arranging them into a logical progression of thought**. It's worth keeping in mind that first (and last) impressions count most. There's a premium, therefore, on your introduction, your conclusion and the first paragraph of your essay. So, after your introduction move to one of your strongest points, quickly getting into the close examination of textual details.

Using the keywords of the question helps to signpost the relevance of your answer and the development of your argument. Though the repetition of keywords can appear a little mechanical if overused, it's particularly helpful in exam conditions.

If the question is 'explore the presentation of family relationships in the poetry of Seamus Heaney', for example, you would need to use phrases such as 'another way in which family relationships are presented...', 'moreover, crucial to the presentation of parent - child relationships...' and 'arguably the most significant relationship is between Heaney and his father...'

Phrases such as 'moreover', 'the most significant / most powerful' and 'the vital example' are especially useful. They **indicate that you have considered a number of examples of the issue at hand, ranked them in terms of their importance** and prioritised the most significant examples. Ideally, of course, you will have gone through this evaluative process. But even if you haven't, such phrases suggest that you have and are therefore helpful as rhetorical tools.

In an overall sense, self-reflection is essential if you are to establish a concise, lucid argument consistently explored in your essay. It can be quite difficult to assess your own work simply by rereading it ("Isn't my genius obvious enough?!") so we would recommend you try the following simple exercise before you submit it. Take a blank sheet of paper (preferably A3) and write your argument at the top of it. Then list in order the main points you have made in your paragraphs. If the list in front of you doesn't remind you of the brilliantly structured argument in your head then you've got some editing to do. This exercise is a really useful way to help you examine the structure of your own argument and assess its structural strengths and logic. **Too often students assume that the links between their discussion and their argument are obvious, mainly because a substantial amount of linking is done in their head**. Unfortunately, examiners can only mark what is on your page, not what may potentially lurk in your brain. So make it easy for them by establishing your argument early and constantly referring back to it as you progress through your essay.

Knowing where you're going and helping the reader: signposting

Imagine your exam essay is a journey on a motorway, with A your point of origin and E your destination. Though you shift lanes from time to time, you'll still be heading in the same direction, hopefully. Along the way, however, you might be tempted to take a slip road at C in order to wander off and explore some extremely interesting landmark or other. Let's imagine getting to this landmark involves taking a number of minor roads and, unfortunately, you don't have a map. And, if you've got one, your satnav's playing up. (And, okay, your phone's got no signal). The danger, clearly, is that if you're not careful, you might get lost finding your way to or back from this arresting detail. Consequently you're not able to return to the motorway in time to continue your journey to point E.

Now switch the close reading of textual detail for the exploration of the interesting landmark. **If you do take the reader off to examine closely a particular feature, then makes sure that you signpost your path clearly.** That way your reader can follow you to the detail and back again, smoothly rejoining the flow of your argument.

Major switches in direction, or moments of transition in your essay also need to be signposted. If you're writing an essay where you need to provide a counter argument, for instance, make sure that the reader doesn't think you've turned back on the journey and started going in the opposite direction. (As on a motorway, this could lead to a nasty collision). If you don't signpost this sort of transition clearly, it will seem to the examiner that you're contradicting yourself.

Consider the following:

Paragraph 1

In his poem 'The Tyger' Blake presents the animal as a figure of awesome beauty and energy as if the poet is enraptured by his vision of it. (the essay goes on to explore textual detail to support this statement)

Paragraph 2

'The Tyger' seems like a terrifying monster, perhaps even an embodiment of evil as evidenced, for example by the poem's hell fire imagery…(goes on to substantiate this point)

As, no doubt, you can imagine, providing clear signposting here is simple. We could add **'But** Blake **also** depicts 'The Tyger' as….' or **'However,** Blake **also** depicts 'The Tyger'…' However, it would be clearer if we demonstrated that we understood the apparent contradiction and could actually explain it. Hence we could start the second paragraph with something like: *Blake's presentation of 'The Tyger' is, however, deeply ambiguous. The imagery of hell, for instance, seems, at first, to contradict the sense of awesome beauty and excitement...'*

Here's a more extended example, based on an entirely imaginary poem.

1. *The poet's imagery in 'X' draws heavily on conventional depictions of pastoral landscapes. For example the gently rolling hills, the sheep, the picturesque classical ruin. X presents us with an almost clichéd image of bucolic calm, an idealised and nostalgic depiction of a conception of a lost Eden.*

2. *The metre of X's poem begins with a regular iambic pattern, giving the reader a sense of conventional balance and order. However, as we move through the poem the metre becomes increasingly irregular, generating an increasing sense of loss of control.*

3. *The theme of the poem is a re-imaging of the fall; the loss of innocence through underlying moral corruption. However X's spin on his theme is to suggest that the seeds of corruption are already buried in this particular notion of Eden. A secondary theme draws our attention to how easily we are deceived by surface appearance, how easily we are lulled into complacency.*

How would you use signposting to improve this switch in tack and show that you know this information seems to be contradictory? (You may also wish to alter the sequence of the paragraphs).

Poor, or no, signposting will make reading your essay a frustrating experience. If you've ever been lost in a car, you'll know how aggravating this will feel for your reader. So, how can we tell if our signposting is wonky? As with setting your line of argument down concisely on one piece of A3 paper, there's a

simple way to check: physically cut up your essay (a copy of it, it goes without saying) into separate paragraphs and then to ask a literary or logical friend to try to put it back in the order you'd intended. If they find this task really difficult, either your signposting isn't clear, or your friend's an incompetent know-nothing fool and you should ask someone with more of a clue.

You can make your essays connect and flow effectively by concluding your paragraphs with a sentence that looks forward to the subject of the following paragraph. So if your next paragraph is going to explain the difference between textual cohesion and textual coherence, then you should end with that.

Cohesion

Cohesion is a term explaining how texts are stuck together by common elements. **A text is cohesive when each bit of it links to some other part of the text.** For example, this sentence is part of a paragraph on the topic of cohesion and the repetition of the key noun 'cohesion' links it in to the previous sentences, a link that is cemented by the phrase 'for example' which indicates that this

sentence will exemplify something in the previous sentence.

What would an incohesive paragraph look like? It would be a series of random non sequiturs, such as the following:

> They'll arrive by one o'clock on Wednesday. Your glasses are looking green. Football is a sport, cricket is an art form. What's on TV tonight? Seamus Heaney is an Irish poet. I prefer white wine, chilled. Look mum, I'm flying.

The really crucial point is that a text can be cohesive, but still be utter drivel. For example,

> This poem is about family relationships. Poems can be about other subjects. Subjects at school should include dragon-taming, instead of food technology. What sort of food would dragons eat? Dragons tend to be rather solitary creatures. Loneliness can be experienced within family. And families are often the subject of poems...

Each sentence in this paragraph is neatly linked into to those around it, is it not? So the paragraph is, strictly speaking, cohesive. But it's also garbage, like the ramblings of a drunk. Improving on this a bit, we get something close to what we call 'quality wittering' on a subject:

> Seamus Heaney's poetry explores family relationships. The most significant relationship, especially in his early poems, is with his father. Heaney's father was a farmer from a long line of farmers. In poems, such as 'Digging' Heaney connects his work as a poet with his father's physical work. Words in Heaney's poems are physical presences. Heaney often uses onomatopoeic effects to bring out this physical quality of language. For example, the 'squelch and slap', 'gravelly ground', 'sucking clabber' or 'thick slobber'...

If we're half-asleep, this might pass for reasonably competent writing. There is some control of the subject and each sentence is linked to the one preceding it. The writing is cohesive. The writer seems to know some decent stuff about Heaney and his poetry. Splash cold water on your face, drink some strong coffee and read more alertly, however, and you'll notice a pervasive **structural looseness**. For instance, notice how the topic of the paragraph slips precipitously from family relationships to Heaney's characteristic sonic imagery.

Topic slippage of this kind is a common weakness in essays. If you find that your paragraph has moved away from its central concern there is a simple way of arresting the slide: **write a final sentence that returns the reader reassuringly back to the topic**:

> *For example, the 'squelch and slap', 'gravelly ground', 'sucking clabber' or 'thick slobber'. Heaney's insistence on this physicality is, in part, born out his anxiety to present writing as analogous to physical labour; his desire is to build a bridge between his intellectual, artistic world and the farming world of his father...*

This is patched up, but it's not perfect. Perhaps the last sentence feels too much like a sleight of hand or clunky switch of gear. It is an improvement though. Better still would be if the paragraph was coherent. Like cohesion, coherence refers to the ways texts are stuck together. Unlike cohesion, **coherence specifically describes how sentences are organised through sense**. If a paragraph is coherent it makes good sense.

> *Seamus Heaney's poetry explores family relationships. The most significant relationship, especially in his early poems, is with his father. Time and again in his poetry, Heaney evokes the figure of his father and of himself, often as a child, somewhat in awe of, and overshadowed by, the large powerful presence. But, while there is admiration, other emotions complicate the picture. A characteristic image, for example, is of his father's 'shoulders globed like a full sail strung' in 'Follower'. Though the atlas image emphasises the father's*

physical power, it also objectifies him, signalling an emotional distance between father and so. The tendency to present his father through physical details is seen again, less flatteringly, in 'Digging' where Heaney comments on 'his straining rump among the flowerbeds'...

Do you agree that this paragraph better than the previous versions? How is it better? If you don't agree, how is it worse? The key difference is that the last example has a much firmer grip on the subject, so that the textual detail quoted backs and supports this central topic. Think of the main topic as the backbone running through your essay.

Another helpful way of thinking of this is that **the topic should appear throughout your essay like the words that run through sticks of roc**k you can buy at English seaside resorts. This spine of words will help make your paragraphs and your whole essay coherent. The textual evidence you employ in each paragraph should relate specifically to this central topic or line of argument, like the sweet candy around the words in the stick of rock.

4. Effective Use of Textual Evidence

There is a clear hierarchy in the use of textual evidence. Imagine it as a 'textual evidence ladder'. At the foot of the ladder is **narrative summary**, or storytelling. This involves summarising the action or content of a text. One rung up from narrative is **description**. Again this focuses on re-telling the story of the text, but here this summary is embellished with some colourful details.

Identification, the third step up, involves a better focus on the techniques used by a writer and less attention to action. At this level, however, features tend to be spotted and labelled. The next step up towards the top is **commentary**, which combines narrative summary with some identification of features of interest and some comments on these. The penultimate rung on the ladder is, of course, **analysis**. Moving into analytical mode means that you are beginning to access the higher grades, from C upwards at A-level.

How is analysis different to identification? When you are analysing a piece of language or a literary device, such as personification, you are seeking to explain how it works, considering why it has been used and the effect it has within the text and upon the reader. Effective analysis entails relating the part you are examining to other aspects of the text. Effective analysis explores the **significance** of textual details. The highest grades go to students who reach the top rung of the ladder, those who can develop and **sustain analysis**. To use exam board speak for a moment, 'A' grade students are able to 'connect detailed critical analysis of significant features to the meanings' in the text and demonstrate 'critical understanding'.

Some examples should help to clarify the picture. For each of the following examples try to identify where it sits on 'the ladder of textual evidence'.

1. *Nick Carraway in 'The Great Gatsby' is a youngish, seemingly honest, man who tells the story of Gatsby. Though he is nowhere near as rich as Gatsby, Nick lives near Gatsby's amazing mansion and is a frequent visitor. Nick is also involved in the story as he falls in love with another character with dubious morals, Jordan Baker.*

2. *After meeting up with the Buchanans, Nick ends up at a flat with Tom, his mistress and some associates. There is a general feeling of unease, exacerbated by the heat and the heavy consumption of alcohol. When his mistress, Myrtle Wilson, annoys Tom he suddenly lashes out, revealing the essential brutality of his character.*

3. *Fitzgerald uses a number of key images to convey the quality of the world in which Gatsby exists. For example, Fitzgerald describes the fruit juice extraction machine and the used up oranges. This is a metaphor for Gatsby's exploitative character.*

4. *After meeting up with the Buchanans, Nick ends up at a flat with Tom's mistress. During the party all the characters get drunk and then things turn rather nasty when his mistress, Myrtle Wilson, annoys Tom he suddenly lashes out and hits her.*

5. *Nick Carraway is both inside and outside the action. He is the narrator, but also a principal character. This double role clearly generates a*

conflict of interest. In telling Gatsby's story, Nick is also telling his own, so we should expect him to be partisan, despite his protestations that he is a truth teller. Our understanding of the story is filtered through and fundamentally shaped by his words and thoughts. Fitzgerald raises questions of the reliability of Nick's narration a number of times. Arguably the most significant examples are the novel's narrative structure, which rearranges the story in a way favourable to Gatsby, Nick's intrusive summative comments on Gatsby being better than the other characters and his emblematic act at Gatsby's funeral of erasing the swear words scrawled on the mansion's steps...

Hopefully, you'll agree that **example 1** is descriptive character summary. The descriptive nature of the writing is signalled by its use of adjectives such as 'youngish', 'amazing' and adjectival phrases such as 'nowhere near as rich as..' and 'with dubious morals'.

Example 2 also is narrative based. But this time there's also some commentary on the atmosphere of the scene and how this is generated.

The writer of **example 3** correctly identifies an important motif in the novel, the repeated images of exploitation. However, in this paragraph they do not develop this observation. So this is an example of identification.

Example 4 is simple narrative. The use of temporal discourse markers are the giveaway clues. If you find yourself repeatedly using words such as 'after', 'during', 'when', 'then', 'next' you know you're writing narrative summary, which is always worth very, very few marks. So don't do it; you're not a novelist, you're a literary critic!

Example 5 In this paragraph the most significant examples are picked up and the analysis is more detailed and developed. This example can look down on the others from somewhere at the top of the ladder; this is sustained analysis.

It should be obvious too that low level responses tend to view the story from the perspective of the characters. **High level responses, by contrast, focus on what the writer is doing and saying and/or the effects of the text on the reader.** In other words, better candidates are more aware of 'how' questions and of the significance of textual details in terms of the communication of meaning.

Earlier we wrote about the limitations of the PEA or PEE formula. Another shortcoming of this GCSE approach is its tendency to promote the examination of single pieces of evidence. Generally when using PEA students make a point, find a quotation to illustrate the point and then write some analysis of the language in the quotations. A major problem with this is that the point relies on only one piece of evidence. Think of your essay as like a speech by a barrister in a court case. You are trying to convince the judge and jury of your argument (think of them as a stubborn, difficult to win over bunch). If you can only supply one piece of evidence your case will probably seem rather weak. Your case will be much stronger if you have a number of good solid pieces of evidence. Flipping this back to a literature essay, if you are arguing that the theme of deception is critical to an understanding of *Macbeth* or if you are arguing that William Blake characteristically combines the abstract with the concrete in his imagery, but you can **only find single examples to support these assertions, it will seem like these are not really significant features of the texts, thus undermining your point**. The judge will be glaring at you over her half-rimmed spectacles and the jury will shift awkwardly in their seats, perhaps muttering something unflattering under their breaths.

Ideally you want to be able to convince your reader through both the weight and detail of your evidence as well as through the sustained acuity of your analysis of it. **Cross-referencing** is a term used to describe linking textual detail from across a text, comparing a quotation for instance from the opening and closing scenes of a play. In *King Lear,* for instance, the king describes himself as a 'dragon' in the opening scene, denoting his sense of his self-mythologising as a mighty, dangerous figure. Later in the play, humbled by his experiences he complains that little dogs 'bark' at him. The animal imagery emphasises both his diminished status and his new self-perception. Using PEA would hamstring your capacity to make this telling, jury and judge-pleasing, type of cross-reference.

Embedding quotations

What's wrong with the use of quotation in the following example?

The tension between the life force and the gravitational pull of death is dramatised in Plath's poetry through her consistent use of colour symbolism:

'Look how white everything is, how quiet, how snowed-in. I am learning peacefulness, lying by myself quietly As the light lies on these white walls, this bed, these hands'.

Here Plath equates whiteness with the ultimate peacefulness of death.

1. Most of the quotation is irrelevant to the point being made.
2. Does the quotation really prove the points being made? Where is the dynamic between life and death? Does the whiteness, as expressed in these lines, simply denote death?
3. The quotation is set out incorrectly.

In general, the convention is that if you are quoting multiple lines of poetry you should set them out as they appear in the poem. In this case the quotation will look like this:

> *'Look how white everything is, how quiet, how snowed-in.*
> *I am learning peacefulness, lying by myself quietly*
> *As the light lies on these white walls, this bed, these hands'.*

Where the lines are cut, what is known technically as their **lineation**, is a fundamental element of what makes them lines of poetry. If you're quoting a short section that overlaps from one line to another use an oblique backwards slash to indicate line endings, as in *'lying by myself quietly / as the light lies on these walls'.*

The most effective way to use quotations is to **take the most important, or the substantive, part from a number of quotations and to put these together embedded within a sentence**. This approach facilitates making connections across a text. Such stitching of textual evidence into your analysis is a tricky art and will take practice to perfect. See below for an example of someone getting to grips with this stitching technique.

> *The tension between the life force and the gravitational pull of death is dramatised in Plath's poetry through her consistent use of colour symbolism. In 'Tulips', for example, whiteness is associated with 'snow' and 'winter' and the obliteration of identity, 'I am nobody'. In contrast, the tulips are associated with the painful feeling of being alive. Plath describes them 'are too red' and 'they hurt me', because her heart is a 'bowl of red blooms'.*

The first set of quotations in the above example work well. But the examples of red imagery are more clumsily incorporated. A simple rule is that when you are embedding quotations within a sentence, **your sentence should still make sense if you remove the quotation marks.** This can clearly be performed in the example below, which, we hope you will agree, exemplifies the skilful incorporation of textual evidence into deft discussion.

> In contrast, the tulips are associated with the painful feeling of being alive. Plath describes the flowers as 'too red', so red, in fact that she is 'hurt' by their colour. The tulips' redness forces her out of her comfortable numbness, making her aware of her emotional pain, her heart, which she describes metaphorically as a 'bowl of red blooms'.

Such considerations of how to use quotations brings us nicely to the topic of close textual analysis.

5. Under the Microscope: Close Analysis of Language

In *King Lear* the King holds a love test to determine which piece of his kingdom each of his daughters will control once he retires from the duties of office. In front of the assembled courtiers, his eldest daughters, Goneril and Regan, are asked by their father to tell him just how much they love him. Both sisters make eloquent speeches in which they declare their utter, undiluted devotion to King Lear. They love him so much that they are, indeed, enemies to all other love (including presumably their love of their husbands).

The third and youngest daughter, Cordelia, listens to her duplicitous, but articulate, sisters in silent horror. And when it comes to her turn, she speaks plainly:

> *'Unhappy that I am, I cannot heave*
> *My heart into my mouth. I love your majesty*
> *According to my bond; no more nor less.'*

If you had to analyse this quotation where would you start?

The most striking and memorable aspect of the language is the metaphorical use of the verb **'heave'**. How different would the sense be if Shakespeare had used 'bring' or 'lift'? 'Heave' is much stronger than either of these alternatives. It suggests the great weight of her feelings and signals the almost physical trial it is for Cordelia to express them. Notice too how the sonic similarities between 'happy', 'heave' and 'heart' emphasise Cordelia's struggle.

Less obviously, there is a proliferation of **personal pronouns** in this short piece of text: 'I' and 'my' appear three times each in just three lines. Is this evidence, perhaps, that something slightly egocentric lies beneath Cordelia's refusal to play Lear's game? Thinking about this further, we might wonder about the exact meaning of 'cannot'. Does this verb mean she is unable to speak? Or that she will not allow herself to? Both meanings are possible. Yet how we read the verb affects how we interpret Cordelia's behaviour. If we accept the second reading, Cordelia is taking a moral stance, refusing to play her father's game, unwilling to exchange empty words for wealth.

Lear certainly reads her blunt 'cannot' as 'will not'. He responds to Cordelia's words by exploding with vitriolic rage at her (as illustrated above).

A fundamental principle underpinning A-level study of English Literature is the influence of contexts on texts. **By applying knowledge of the play's context to this quotation we can open up further avenues for close analysis**. We can put this quotation into the wiser context of the play itself. For example, the issue of articulate lying versus inarticulate attempts to express the truth is a fundamental concern of the play. We could, therefore, cross-reference Cordelia's lines with others from later in the play. *King Lear* is also a play about the loosening of an essentially medieval way of thinking - in which respect was based on authority, power and duty - and the emergence of a new way of thinking where respect is predicated on what we do. Hence the word 'bond' resonates throughout the play. 'Bond' here means duty, but it also suggests bondage or being bound. This raises the issue of what is the duty of a daughter to her father, especially if her father is capricious, cruel and potentially tyrannical. Why, after all, should Cordelia play this contrived and loaded game in which empty words are exchanged for wealth? Effective close reading, then, happens when we stop and examine the language intensely, rather than skimming over its implications. We are used to reading quickly when we read texts or search on the internet. **In works of literature, language is used more carefully and artfully, so we need to slow down**

and consider how the medium influences the message, how the way something is said affects what is said. To see a superb close textual analysis of poetry go to chapter 22 (in Part the Fourth).

For your close analysis to be conveyed effectively you need to write well. Hence in the next section of the book our attention will turn from reading to writing.

6. Good Writing

What does good essay writing look like? What makes writing bad, ugly or ineffective?

Of course, there aren't absolute hard and fast rules about the distinction between good and bad essay writing. **Like clothing style, to some extent determining whether writing is good or bad is an aesthetic judgement, dependent on taste**.

Nevertheless, we can establish some its key features. Like the style in the visuals here it is quickly apparent what is good style and what is not. Good writing certainly aids communication, for example. Good writing is also economical and direct and avoids clumsy repetitions. In fact we can identify other major indicators of good essay writing by considering vocabulary, sentence construction and register.

Vocabulary

As well as having energy and vigour, good writing, for example, is expressed accurately, with correct punctuation, grammar and spelling. **Technical accuracy is important in its own right, but its main function is as an aid to communication**. Errors in grammar or punctuation confuse meaning. Think, for example, of how the absence of commas in 'I like cooking my family and my pets' impacts on the meaning of the sentence.

"A woman, without her man, is nothing."
"A woman: without her, man is nothing."
Punctuation is powerful.

Ⓖ Grammarly Cards

A surprisingly high number of A-level candidates cannot spell key technical terms that should have been mastered at GCSE, such as 'simile', 'metaphor' and 'onomatopoeia'. More specifically A-level vocabulary, such as 'tragedy', 'omniscient' and 'soliloquy' are often spelt in highly imaginative, but incorrect ways in A-level exams. It is therefore well worth the effort ensuring that you understand fully, and can spell accurately, the key terms of literary study.

A developed critical vocabulary is a key indicator of a high quality essay and it will be one of the first things examiners notice. So make a conscious effort to develop your critical vocabulary. In addition to the commonly used terminology, find out, for instance, about more exotic terms, such as 'prolepsis' and 'analepsis', 'stichomythia', 'hamartia', 'hendiadys', 'antithesis', 'zeugma' or 'collocation'. (A list of critical terminology appears in the glossary at the end of this book.)

Sentences

Another area of common errors is in the writing of sentences. What is a sentence exactly? Quite a few students think a sentence is defined by starting with a capital letter and ending with a full stop. Hence they present sentence fragments as if they are full sentences. Like we have done with this one.

Here are some frequent errors:

1. *Which shows that Chaucer is satirising the church authorities.*
2. *Making it difficult to know whether we should sympathise or not with Frankenstein's creature.*
3. *Whereas Hamlet is unable to complete his revenge because he thinks about it too much.*
4. *Illustrating Emily Dickinson's complex and unusual imagery.*
5. *Hamlet is obsessed with Claudius's guilt Claudius is obsessed with Hamlet's erratic behaviour.*
6. *Frankenstein does not deserve our sympathy, his actions are*

motivated by vanity and self-interest.

Each of the first four examples is not a grammatically correct sentence because it does not have a subject. In example 1 we don't know what it is that 'shows' Chaucer's attitude. In example 2, we don't know what makes the question of our sympathy difficult. In the third example a conjunction is used, but we only have one half of the comparison. Either there should be a subject before the 'whereas' (perhaps 'Laertes sweeps to revenge his father') or after the 'too much'. In the fourth example, we don't know what example illustrates Dickinson's characteristic imagery.

So, **a sentence has to have as a minimum a subject and a finite verb**. 'The man ran' is therefore a sentence. 'The running man...' isn't, because here the verb is functioning as an adjective. Often a sentence will also need an object to be complete. The subject does the action of the verb; the object is acted upon. So, in 'the man threw the ball' the man is the subject, the ball the object.

A sentence can stand alone and make sense. That is why technically it is called an independent main clause. In contrast, clauses that do not have a subject and a finite verb are dependent on a sentence to make sense. For example, 'in the middle of the play' is a dependent clause because it doesn't have a verb. 'In the middle of the play Lear's inner turmoil is made external through the storm on the heath' is a sentence.

The fifth example is of what is called **a 'fused sentence'**. Basically this means that two separate sentences have been incorrectly put together. This mistake could be corrected through a full stop, a semi-colon or through adding a conjunction:

> *Hamlet is obsessed with Claudius's guilt, whereas Claudius is obsessed with Hamlet's erratic behaviour.*

What about the last example? This is called **a 'sentence splice'**. This time two separate sentences have been incorrectly joined with a comma between them. A full stop, semi-colon or conjunction could be used here. We would use a semicolon or a conjunction as the second sentence is illustrating the point made in the first:

Frankenstein does not deserve our sympathy; his actions are motivated by vanity and self-interest.

Frankenstein does not deserve our sympathy because his actions are motivated by vanity and self-interest

Sometimes loss of control of clauses can lead to a lack of clarity. Look at this mangled monstrosity taken from our book on writing GCSE Literature essays:

In this poem, written by Yeats at the start of the twentieth century, in response to both personal and political events, Yeats, who was an Irish writer from an Anglo-Irish background, uses a number of familiar images.

Or this one, like a multiple pile-up on a motorway:

Mary Shelley's Frankenstein, *first published in 1818 at a time of great political and social turmoil resulting from the aftermath of the French Revolution in 1789 and the subsequent cracking down on dissent in England, is a Gothic novel presenting different aspects of both the creature, often referred to as the 'monster' somewhat unfairly by*

46

Frankenstein, and its creator, Frankenstein himself, making it difficult for the reader to distinguish clearly who she (Shelley) would like the reader to think of as the hero and who should be the villain of the novel.

Three simple rules will help avoid this sort of mistake.
- Firstly try to keep your subject and verb as close together as possible.
- Secondly strip out clauses within clauses, such as *'a time of great political turmoil...resulting from the aftermath...'*
- Thirdly aim for one idea per sentence.

For instance, the first sentence of the second example would be better as:

> *First published in 1818 at a time of great political and social turmoil, Mary Shelley's 'Frankenstein' is a Gothic novel presenting different aspects of both the creature and his creator.*

Though we've neatened it up, with this improved version we would still want to know how the first detail of the socio-historical setting is relevant to the presentation of the central protagonists.

Remember the essential thing you are after is clarity of communication. Keep your sentences clear and economical. It is the quality of your ideas that really counts.

Currently examination boards assess the quality of writing under AO1. The **criteria for a top grade answer** are:
- *consistently fluent and accurate writing in appropriate register*
- *critical terminology accurately and consistently used*
- *well-structured, coherent and detailed argument consistently developed*

So far we've covered fluency, structure, detail, argument, critical terminology and accuracy. Next we'll explore what is meant by 'an appropriate register'.

Register

Here's what we said about register in the GCSE version of this book:

> Imagine you have an interview for a job you really want. How do you dress? If you're sensible you will, of course, dress smartly. Turning up to a formal interview dressed casually in your old beach shorts, some flip-flops and a pair of sunglasses would probably not be very helpful.
>
> Formal writing style is the equivalent of dressing smartly, of showing you're taking the task seriously. To write formally means not using slang or other forms of non-standard English. It means not abbreviating, not using colloquialisms or txt speech. Often in life we adapt the language we use to the situation we're in. The better we can do this usually the more successful we are going to be. Think of the language you use with your friends, or that you might use to a baby, or to a pet. If you used this language to a judge or a policeman you might find yourself in trouble: *'Who's a lovely lickle policeman, then, who's a lovely lickle boy? Yes, you are....yes you know you are....'*

This advice holds true for A-level Literature essays too. In fact it is even more **important at this level that you adopt a suitable formal academic style**.

Writing *'King Lear goes totally ape shit and loses his head big time when he's like dissed in front of his homies by Cordelia'* is not going to exactly endear you to examiners. However right your point is, if you write like this (which we suspect is highly unlikely) you haven't shown that you've learnt to express it in the appropriate academic formal style.

Your teachers may have told you not to use the personalised voice in academic essays. By this we mean that you shouldn't write 'I think that..' or 'I believe that'. Such phrases sound naive because they are redundant - your whole essay is supposed to express your own ideas in response to a question. **Writing in a 'depersonalised voice' will also make your writing sound more assured, confident and authoritative**.

Compare, *'I think that Plath uses red colour symbolism to convey the sense that life is vital and exciting, but also painful and potentially dangerous'* with, *'Plath's use of red colour symbolism conveys the sense that life is vital and exciting, but also painful and potentially dangerous'*. The latter sounds much more like academic writing. But this is not to say you should never use the personal 'I' voice. Used sparingly it can be powerful, expressing your confidence in your own critical voice. Save it for when you're going out on an interpretive limb, when you're expressing something individual, or when you're disagreeing with someone else's opinions. You may also want to use the personal voice in your conclusion to make your final position on the subject clear. Professor Richard Marggraf-Turley in his useful book *Writing Essays* puts it like this, *'using the first person allows you to 'step-out- of the essay to speak more directly to the reader, and also to inject a human dimension to the discussion'*.

7. Assessment Objectives

After the introduction of the new A-Level specification [for first teaching in September 2015] all the exam boards will use the same five assessment objectives. As we've already said, you should write with these assessment objectives in mind, but not aim to tick each one off. It's also important that you are aware of the weighting of the AOs on specific modules. Most modules test two or three of the AOs and sometimes a specific AO is double-weighted. In practice this will mean examiners mark your work and then check it against the requirements of the double-weighted AOs. They will generally only use the secondary AOs to determine where you fit in a band.

> *AO1: articulate informed, personal and creative responses to literary texts using associated concepts and terminology, and coherent, accurate written expression*

> *AO2: analyse ways in which meanings are shaped in literary texts by poetic, narrative or dramatic devices*

> *AO3: demonstrate understanding of the significance and influence of the contexts in which literary texts are written and received*

> *AO4: explore connections and comparisons between different literary texts*

> *AO5: explore literary texts informed by different interpretations*

Exam boards also provide descriptions of A/B and E/U borderline work measured against the assessment objectives. We won't repeat here all the relevant information as it is easily available on the boards' websites or in their specifications. If you don't know which exam board's specification you are studying find out and make sure you read the key documents, especially the specification mark schemes. Most exam boards publish guidance on coursework, exemplar materials, past papers, mark schemes and Chief Examiner's reports. All these are really useful sources of information and can, and should, be skim read quickly. **Don't assume your teachers will do this for you, take responsibility yourself**.

Okay, so we've dealt now with most of the features of successful essays we identified in the introduction. We've picked up the desirability of your work being interesting and referred to demonstrating some original, independent thought. That leaves us with #7 'using contexts effectively', #11 'using other interpretations' and #9 'writing effective introductions and conclusions'. As we're going to explain how to use contexts and different interpretations later in the sections on writing about poetry, prose and drama, the next section will guide you through the often underrated art of introductions and conclusions.

8. Introductions and Conclusions

Introductions

What are the features of a good introduction? Perhaps before we ask that question we should consider the function of an introduction to an English literature essay.

Sometimes students think of an introduction as a sort of warm-up, a gentle first sentence or two breaking the writer and the reader into the essay. These sorts of warm-up sentences often start with the repetition of the information in the title - 'In this essay I am going to write about the presentation of gender and gender relationships in *The Bloody Chamber* by Angela Carter. Another common tactic is to provide some contextual information: 'Angela Carter wrote *The Bloody Chamber* in 1979 during a period of radical political and social change in British society'.

What's wrong with the second example? Nothing, if this detail about the socio-historical setting is important to the issue to be discussed in the essay. Another couple of simple rules - start with the most important points and only use context when it helps to explain these most important points. If *The Bloody Chamber* essay is going to go on to relate the election of the first female Prime Minister to the often radical presentation of gender in Carter's work, or if the candidate is going to link radical political change to the idea of transformation in *The Bloody Chamber* then this opening with socio-historical context would be justified.

In the introduction to your essay **the most important thing you need to establish is your line of argument or thesis**. Contextualising the issue and the text is useful, through reference to literary context, such as genre, or to socio-historical context. It is also good idea to provide an overview of the issue at hand and to write a programmatic statement in which you signpost how your essay will be structured. For example, you might finish your introduction with something along the lines of 'the issue of gender will be explored by examining Carter's presentation of characters, character relationships and through the settings of her stories.' The reader knows then that the next paragraph will be focused on characterisation.

Remember too that examiners and teachers are human and have other things to do with their time. Try to make them want to read your essay. **A clear, engaging style and the sort of unusual slant on a question we've recommended will certainly help hook your reader**.

Have a look at the following four introductions. To what extent do they fulfil the criteria above? The first example is from a timed A2 examination practice essay exploring how the audience is made to feel uneasily complicit with the plotting of Iago in Shakespeare's *Othello*.

> *1.* Othello *is a play about a black general in the Venetian army who secretly marries a privileged young white woman, Desdemona. After they're married, Othello's best friend and confidant, Iago, plots against him, making the general believe that Desdemona has been unfaithful to him with Cassio. Despite her innocence, Othello believes Iago and eventually murders his wife, only to find out in the end that Iago has tricked him. We never really know why Iago does this, which is way his actions have been described as caused by 'motiveless malignancy'.*

Clearly this is narrative summary. There is very little sense of the question or of how the narrative information provided might be relevant to how the audience responds to Iago. If the student had gone on to say that the narrative encourages us to sympathise with the guiltless Desdemona and perhaps with the deceived Othello, things would have been a bit better. As it stands this introduction would be worth very few marks.

The second example is from an A2 coursework essay on Arthur Miller's *The Crucible* and is answering a question on the presentation of religion in the play.

> *2. Starting with alleged communists employed by the American government, between 1950 and 1954 Senator Joseph McCarthy conducted a 'witch-hunt' for communist spies in America society. The idea of communist spies buried in all walks of American life was a terrifying one for the American people. Suddenly anyone could be a spy: Your next door neighbour, the teacher at your child's school, your best friend. McCarthy attempted to create a 'pure' America through show trials, forcing confessions and by blackmailing defendants into revealing the names of supposed communists. Failure to comply with McCarthy's committee was punishable by law, just as in the* **The Crucible** *the judges charge Giles Corey with contempt. Though it was on a smaller scale, the principles underpinning the witch-hunt in Salem were the same as those underlying what became known as McCarthyism. Miller thus protested against McCarthyism through analogy to the hysteria and injustice of the historical witch-hunts.*

This is much better than the first example. What are the strengths of this introduction? It's well-written, clear and direct; it certainly shows a good knowledge and understanding of the socio-historical context; towards the end this context is also related effectively to the play being studied.

What are its weaknesses? If we hadn't told you the title would you have been able to work out what theme this essay is focusing on? **There's a lot of context here, too much in fact, because it is not sufficiently linked to the question under consideration**. It feels a bit as if the context has been put in to fulfil the context assessment objective, rather than being employed to help explain the central concern. What is this student actually arguing about the play and its presentation of religion?

This third example is the introduction to an A2 coursework essay on the extent to which the structure of David Mitchell's *Cloud Atlas* is integral to the novel's themes.

> 3. *David Mitchell's postmodernist novel* Cloud Atlas *tells six different stories in six different genres of writing. Each story dramatises a struggle between the story's protagonist and the oppressive societies within which they live. Though the location shifts from Belgium to New Zealand and the temporal setting spans from the nineteenth century to a distant post-apocalyptic future, and though the stories are also written in different genres, the DNA of each story remains essentially the same. Mitchell has likened the structure of his novel to a Russian Doll, with each story embedded in another one, so that 'every possible moment is contained in this moment, regressing to infinity'. The repetitive and symmetrical structure - the second half of the novel is a mirror image of the first - thus reinforces the novel's central concern about the endurance of the human spirit within an oppressive context.*

Once again, this is a well-written introduction, clear and easy to follow. This time there is no use of socio-historical context. Some literary context is suggested through the term 'postmodernist' though this is not explained or developed. In this example the student does have **a clear line of argument, or thesis**, which is that the structure is indeed integral to what they read as the novel's central theme. It might have been better to start with a point about the novel's structure, but though it's not perfect, this is a very good introduction.

The final example is from another timed exam practice essay, this time for AS, on the presentation of suffering in Mary Shelley's novel *Frankenstein*.

4. Mary Shelley's novel, **Frankenstein** - *the tale of the Promethean overreacher - encapsulates the best in the potential of humanity, and the worst. The characters of 'Frankenstein' fall victim to suffering - either as a result of their own actions, or the actions of someone dear to them. Indeed, Shelley's own life was filled with suffering; she lost two of her children and she became a widow at the age of just 25. In addition,* **Paradise Lost** *and 'The Rime of the Ancient Mariner' both include suffering, which leads to 'the suffering of characters' being 'directed by narratives outside of 'Frankenstein', in the words of Andrew Green. Though these texts have a great effect on the novel, in its own right, 'Frankenstein' is a story of suffering on a great scale, affecting all of its characters, and their suffering is, to some extent deserved.*

So over to you! How good an introduction is this? Consider what it is trying to do and how it does this by considering both its strengths and weaknesses.

We would classify this as a strong A grade introduction because:

1. There's a firm grip on the subject of suffering with some ideas ventured about the ways in which this is presented. For instance, the extent to which the characters are the authors of their own suffering.

2. Various contexts are neatly brought to bear on the topic: autobiographical information about Mary Shelley; literary context about the influence of other seminal texts; a helpful quotation from a critic, Andrew Green.

3. The introduction arrives at its thesis in the final sentence.

4. As a whole, the introduction is expressed clearly and concisely, qualities especially important in exam conditions.

Conclusions

The most common problem with conclusions is that they merely repeat the

content of the introduction or, in the dullest cases, the exact wording of the question. How can we avoid this problem? One way is to **think of your essay as equivalent to a scientific experiment**. In your introduction you put forward your argument or hypothesis. In the main body of the essay you analyse the data closely to see if your hypothesis is correct or whether it needs refining in some way. As we 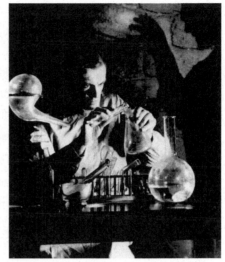 said earlier, writing is a form of thinking, so it wouldn't be surprising if you discovered some new thoughts in the process of writing your essay.

In your conclusion you should weigh up the key points you've examined. Try to express these key points in your argument succinctly. **Your conclusion then can confidently either confirm the hypothesis, or put forward a refinement of it in the light of the evidence you've analysed. In either case, make sure you make your final position on the question clear to the reader**.

An open, exploratory approach to essay writing makes the experience much more interesting to write (and read) than an explanation of an already completely settled view. Being prepared to change your ideas also indicates that you are trying to analyse the data fairly and objectively. The overall effect of adopting this approach is to make your essays lively and engaging.

Some people like to end their essay with a neat summative quotation, others prefer to hold back a strong point to finish on. Either or both can work. It is, however, useful to **try in your conclusion to step back a little from the**

question and the issue at hand, perhaps thinking in terms of its significance in wider cultural discourse. It can also be useful to consider any weaknesses in the methodology you've used. Finally, if your essay really has been exploratory you may have discovered **some new questions and avenues for investigation** worthy of further investigation.

Read the following conclusions and decide on how successful you think they are. Obviously it's a little artificial to do this without reading the rest of the essays, but you should still be able to tell whether these are any good or not. The first comes from an AS exam essay exploring the presentation of the theme of change in W.B.Yeats's poem 'The Wild Swans at Coole', the second from an A2 piece assessing whether Cormac McCarthy's novel *The Road* is anything more than a 'zombie film in fine prose'.

> *1. To conclude, it seems that Yeats's poem 'The Wild Swans at Coole' portrays change as fundamentally positive. Yet the characteristic ambivalence of Yeats is evinced by the poem's acknowledgements of its potentially negative impact, particularly the sense of the poet's own mortality, as symbolised by the swans' flight at the end of the poem. Change itself relates to Yeats' own life at this time as well as to his writing style, the latter of which was evolving as he wrote this poem. Here the poet combines his earlier mysterious 'Celtic Twilight' style with a less sonorous, more modern, outward looking and more objective style. The Celtic heroes, for example, are replaced by the swans. Yet these 'brilliant creatures' are also new avatars of the Celtic heroes. Thus Yeats' characteristically combines change with continuity, hope with despair.*

> *2. The quotation in my title discredits the zombie horror film genre as one not worth examining. Yet it fails to take into account that zombie films are often vehicles for the exploration of important ideas, such as free will and self determination, or the nature of the consumerism they satirise. McCarthy's decision to base his novel on this patronised genre is not unusual in the context of the rest of his work. His artistic*

enterprise involves taking typical pieces of American popular culture, such as Westerns or Zombie films and re-imagining them through a realist perspective. In **The Road** *McCarthy adapts the genre and its cinematography, unpicking the cultural understanding of these films, breathing new life into well worn motifs, including most significantly that of the road itself.*

One of the things that must be revealed to you is that the introductions of most literary texts are often rewritten several times. Writers draft and re-draft until they are happy with what they've written. It is the same for writing essays and it really is no surprise. Intellectual exploration often brings you to unexpected destinations; destinations that modify your overall understanding of a topic. **Such reshaping of your writing must be embraced as the positive it is, rather than being viewed as a waste of time.** First drafts of essays tend to be where ambitions are fulfilled and often result in interesting though not necessarily the most focused discussion. Be prepared to bin some of your most loved work, especially if it doesn't contribute very much to your intended hypothesis. The drafting process is vital in ensuring that your essays are sleek, efficient and devastating.

9. The Drafting Process

Planning

Before you write the first draft of your essay **it is vital that you produce an essay plan** or outline. Your essay plan should emerge from the brainstorming you do in response to the question and involve focusing on the key material generated during brainstorming and re-ordering this into a logical sequence. For coursework essays it's a good idea to write a **one paragraph synopsis**, outlining your line of argument and the direction your essay will take. While you don't have to stick to this synopsis when you write your first draft it will provide a useful route map through the process of writing.

Effective essay writing is a process and you need to be prepared to change, edit, even discard some of your writing. For your coursework it's essential that you produce a number of drafts. Your teachers will mark your first full draft in detail, but you should also write a few versions yourself first and edit these on a word processor. Our advice is to write your first draft fairly quickly in a few sections. Rather than writing the opening and then starting to edit it, it's better to press on so that you have the whole essay at least in rough form. **Rewriting the introduction will be easier once you've completed the rest of the essay**.

Proofread carefully to see if you any words out. ~Author Unknown

It sounds obvious, but **you must proofread to check for technical accuracy**. Don't assume that a computer spell checker will pick up all errors - it won't because these programmes are not able to take context into account. The sentence 'do knot rely two much up on a spell-chequer' would not be corrected!

As you read over your first draft pay special attention to whether each paragraph is clearly relevant to your line of argument. **If some paragraphs seem to be digressing, either cut them or bring them back to the central concerns through reference to the keywords of the question.** Check too that you've used a substantial amount of textual evidence. As a rule of thumb the fewer quotations there are in an essay the weaker it usually is. Ensure that these quotations are relevant to the points you're making and that you stop and explore the implications of the writer's specific use of language and literary techniques.

The assessment objectives for each module are published in the exam 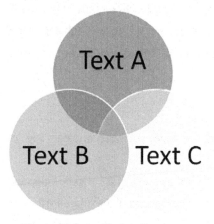 board's specifications, so it would be sensible to check these. If, for example, there's a substantial chunk of marks for the quality of your comparison, you will need to use clear comparative discourse markers, such as 'in contrast', 'similarly', 'however' and so forth. Remember though, that it will be the quality and sophistication of your comparison that will earn you marks. Saying two poems are alike because they're both pre-1914 or that two plays are similar because they both feature female characters will earn zero marks. **Look especially for surface similarities that on closer inspection reveal important differences.**

Ensure that your essay is balanced. Is there a reasonable amount of detail on all the texts or does one text dominate? It's unlikely that an essay structure consisting a couple of sides on text A followed by two sides on text B and the same for text C will help you to write comparatively. If you have chosen a structure in which you write about one text per paragraph, make sure that you switch between these texts regularly. If you've written more than two paragraphs in a row on one of your texts you may need to rearrange your paragraphs.

As suggested earlier, **try cutting up your essay and giving it to someone else to put back together**. If they can't do this (assuming they're a competent reader) you need to improve your signposting.

Once you've written a complete first draft leave it for a day or two before going over it. This will help give you some critical distance. **Try to read your essay through a stranger's eyes**. Try objectively to identify its strengths and weaknesses. Sometimes you will find yourself reluctant to cut a section, perhaps because you know it's well-written or because it concerns something you're confident you've mastered, even though you know it's not strictly relevant to your question or that it repeats a point you've already established. This is natural and understandable. But you've got to be ruthless - **cut anything that is not directly contributing to the development of your argument**.

In summary, check the following carefully:
- your introduction and conclusion - have you got a clear line of argument?
- your use of textual evidence - is there enough of it? Does it support your points? Have you analysed the implications of the language?
- the technical accuracy of your writing - don't lose marks through carelessness.
- do your paragraphs flow? do they start with topic sentences which advance the discussion?
- the structure - is there a good balance of material on the texts? Is your comparison clear and well considered? Is your essay well signposted?
- have you addressed the AOs? do you need to include contexts and/or other readers' interpretations?
- the quality of your expression. Cut any redundant words and check that your sentences are clear and uncluttered.

How long should your essay be? Obviously this depends on a number of contexts, such as the size of your handwriting and whether you're writing an exam or coursework essay. Exam boards set word limits for coursework. For an exam about four sides should be long enough. **Busy examiners definitely don't want to read long, unfocused and rambling essays**.

Professor Maggraf Turley's advice on essay length in *Writing Essays* is worth remembering:

> *'The little tag you are given to join two answer booklets together in exams is an object of loathing for markers, and prompts their automatic nervous systems to twitch in despair whenever one is seen'.*

So avoid such involuntary loss of motor control in examiners by making your essay focused and to the point. Making it a brilliant read will also ease their jerky reflexes but you should know this already.

Such shameless borrowing from an established expert to reinforce our own point brings us nicely to the quite technical yet essential city-state of referencing and its dark underbelly, plagiarism.

10. Plagiarism and Referencing

According to the Oxford English Dictionary to **plagiarise** is to 'take and use the thoughts, writings, inventions, etc. of another person as one's own'. Wikipedia defines plagiarism as **'wrongful appropriation'** and with the quaintly archaic verb 'purloining', meaning stealing, of other people's words and ideas. If we had not put quotation marks around the above and hadn't acknowledged the source of this information we would have been guilty of plagiarism.

Unless you're a genius, it is unlikely that you will develop completely original and groundbreaking criticism about a text and it is important that you **remember that your interpretation will lie in a field of previous interpretations**. So don't be tempted to be 'original' by borrowing someone else's intellectual hard sweat! It is usually not a good fit and more often than not can be spotted easily by your teacher.

Deliberate plagiarism is a very serious act of intellectual theft and attempted deception. Anyone caught plagiarising in their coursework essays will be awarded zero marks for this work and the offence may impact on the rest of their qualifications in that subject.

Plagiarism extends from copying a few sentences to copying paragraphs to submitting an entire essay written by someone other than yourself. The worst plagiarists brazenly copy and paste from another source - the change in style and complexity of thought usually gives it away though. Sometimes plagiarism can be accidental, the result of poor referencing of sources. You can **avoid plagiarism simply by using quotation marks around any sentences from other writers** and through acknowledging their contribution in your footnotes and/or bibliography. In fact it's doubly stupid not to do this as you'd actually earn marks for showing you've read and applied what other readers have said about your texts!

So the moral of the lesson is: acknowledge the ideas of those people you have read, it will probably boost your overall mark.

Referencing

So how do you acknowledge your debt to previous intellectual pioneers? Through **referencing**. Referencing is simply the cataloguing of the various people you have read and whose ideas you have drawn upon to complete your own personal exploration of a literary text. There are two

main sources of referencing. One is what might be described as textual referencing i.e. direct quotation from a critic. So for example, if you were writing an essay on Pat Barker's *Regeneration* and how gender stereotypes are challenged by World War One, you might use John Brannigan as follows:

> *Barker presents an Edwardian world where gender is no longer what is used to be. What was once familiar and reliable has now been distorted into threatening new shapes.* John Brannigan astutely

recognises that "the transgression of gender and sexual codes is usually shown to be debilitating rather than emancipatory."

Hence it is very clear that you are using material that is not yours and whose material it is. It is also a good idea to show where exactly you have found this material, so you would refine the above example to:

> Barker presents an Edwardian world where gender is no longer what is used to be. What was once familiar and reliable has now been distorted into threatening new shapes. John Brannigan astutely recognises that "the transgression of gender and sexual codes is usually shown to be debilitating rather than emancipatory, (*Pat Barker*, 99)."

This tells us that the quotation you have used comes from page 99 of Brannigan's book *Pat Barker*. If you were weaving elements of this quotation into your own sentence, then your referencing would look like this:

> Barker presents an Edwardian world where gender is no longer what is used to be. What was once familiar and reliable has now been distorted into threatening new shapes. Her nuanced interrogation of gender as well as her historian's allegiance to veracity mean that "the transgression of gender and sexual codes" does not suggest a simplistic or misleadingly utopian development; Sarah Lumb's liberation is only temporary and ultimately becomes "debilitating rather than emancipatory," (Brannigan, *Pat Barker*, 99).

The effect is always the same: **your discussion is uniquely your own but it is driven by the ideas of others, who you are gracious enough to acknowledge.** If you refer to Brannigan's work repeatedly you may need to abbreviate so your reference looks like this (Brannigan, *PB*, 99) after the first time you refer to this critical text. Ultimately, you must acknowledge the author, the work and the page number and in this order. **Even if you are paraphrasing another person's ideas you are still using someone else's**

work; in this case you must still acknowledge the ideas but you will not use speech marks in your text.

In general, we recommend that this is the extent of the detail that you supply about other sources. Endless footnotes and endnotes are distracting and if the material is that important it really should be in the main body of your essay. The end of your essay is where you compile a full list of all critical works you have referred to in your essay. This list is called a **bibliography**. One way of thinking  about bibliographies is that they are receipts that detail the intellectual ideas

 you have purchased in preparation for your essay. (You probably won't feel as distressed as the lady above). You could also compare it to a list of ingredients that you consult before baking. It tells you everything that went into the mixing bowl but it will not tell you what the finished product will taste like.

Bibliographies are very useful indicators of the quality of an essay. **The longer the bibliography, generally the better the essay** as it will demonstrate an in depth research of the text, critical responses to this text and awareness of contextual factors. However, you should only list those sources that you draw on directly in your essay. A half-heard conversation in a Parisian cafe probably shouldn't be included or your traumatising experiences playing "Call of Duty"! You may read a wide range of texts in preparation for your essay but you don't need to list these unless you specifically use their ideas. It might be tempting to flesh out your bibliography to gigantic proportions but be sensible; keep it simple and functional.

If you only have Barker's *Regeneration* listed in your bibliography you should be concerned; it implies that you have not taken the time to explore the various critical responses to the novel nor have you conducted much research on the topic you are exploring. At A-level, it is crucial that you are aware of these critical responses and find your own position in this field of discourse.

A bibliography for an essay on *Regeneration* might look as follows:

Bibliography

Balaev, Michelle. *The Nature of Trauma in American Novels.* Northwestern University Press, 2012.

Barker, Pat. *Regeneration.* Penguin, 1991.

Barry, Peter. *Beginning Theory, 3rd Edition.* Manchester University Press, 2009.

Brannigan, John. *Orwell to the Present: Literature in England 1945 - 2000.* Palgrave, 2002.

---. *Pat Barker.* Manchester University Press, 2005.

Fussell, Paul. *The Great War and Modern Memory.* Oxford University Press, 1970.

Monteith, Sharon. *Pat Barker.* Northcote House, 2002.

Tylee, Claire M.. *The Great War and Women's Consciousness.* University of Iowa Press, 1990

Westman, Karin E.. *Regeneration: A Reader's Guide.* Continuum, 2001.

You will notice that each entry is put in alphabetical order and always in the same format:

Author's name - title of text - publishing house - year of publication

"---" simply means that it's another publication by the same author, in this case John Brannigan.

For a chapter in a collection of essays it would take this form:

> Brown, Dennis. "The Regeneration Trilogy: Total War, Masculinities, Anthropologies and the Talking Cure." *Critical Perspectives on Pat Barker*. Eds. Sharon Monteith et al. University of South Carolina, 2005. 187-202.

To reference an online article, in this case one discussing homosexuality in "Regeneration," you would use this format:

> Swann, D. *An Unexpected Message from our Past*. www.k-state.edu, 2004.
>
> http://www.kstate.edu/english/westmank/regeneration/homosexuallty.s wann.html [22 July 2015]

The general format is:

> **Author's name - title of text - publishing website- year of publication - full web address - date article was accessed**

It may often be the case that the author of online material is unspecified. In this case you specify the website in your main text and your bibliography entry looks like this.

> *Regeneration (novel)*. Wikipedia, 2015.
>
> http://en.wikipedia.org/wiki/Regeneration_(novel) [22 July 2015]

It might seem like a load of complicated claptrap, but referencing is a vital skill in essay writing and you need to do it whether you like it or not. The exam boards specify it as a requirement and it is a surefire way of avoiding any accidental plagiarism. Once you get the hang of it, it becomes second nature and will become a very useful skill when going on to university study. **Make sure that you check whether there is a specific referencing system specified by your exam board or university**. There are several different systems, all slightly different but ultimately adhering to the same basic principle. Now that the administrative requirements have been covered it's on to the fun stuff.

PART THE SECOND
WRITING ABOUT SPECIFIC
Types Of Text

PART THE SECOND: Writing About Specific Types of Text

In this section we want to turn away from the mechanics of writing brilliant literature essays and consider the reading process that must take place before any writing is done. **Reading in this sense is more than just reading words on the page; it is a quest for textual meaning.** As should be obvious from the driving philosophy behind our book, there is no off-the-shelf formula to achieve this. It is a subjective and highly personal process that is unique to every reader as every reader comes with a uniquely complex value system and approach to searching for textual meaning.

How would you arrange following terms to represent visually the relationship between them?

READER – TEXT – MEANING – CRITIC - AUTHOR

Which term is, for you, the most and least important?

Traditionally the 'meaning' of a literary text was understood to be created by its writer who implanted it into his or her text. The job of the reader was to develop the advanced reading skills necessary to extract and decode this authoritative meaning. The reader would be aided in this process through training by an oracle, a high priest of truth; also known as a literary academic. This hierarchy can be visualised as follows:

In the 1960s this model began to be challenged; most radically by the French cultural theorist, Roland Barthes. Barthes overturned the idea that the author controls the single authoritative 'meaning' of a text. Instead, **all texts have many meanings and, crucially, these meanings, he argued, are created not by the author, but by the reader**. In Barthes' radical rearrangement the reader sits comfortably top of the pile while the author is not only toppled but banished to the oblivion of irrelevance.

But did Barthes go too far? Is the author really, as he famously claimed, dead? Have we no say in or control over the meaning of what we are writing now? If so, why write at all? When you speak, you're the author of your words, aren't you? If somebody misunderstands what you say is their interpretation of your meaning more valid than your own? Surely not.

Influenced by thinkers such as Barthes, modern approaches to literature emphasise the creative role of the reader in generating the meanings of a text. But, broadly, there is a consensus that these **meanings are produced through the relationship between the writer's words and the reader's reading of them**. In short, the relationship is interactional and continually evolving, as shown below.

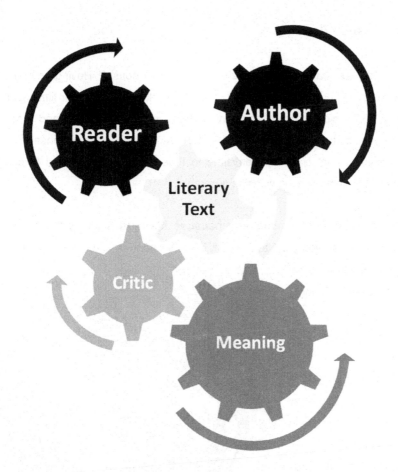

Literary
Text

So think of yourself as a 'centre of meaning', or at least, a centre of meaning-making. Your role in reading a text is not as a passive recipient, but as an active creator of meanings. **In short, reading is a creative act.** Or to be more specific, it is a series of ongoing acts of creations as each successive reader actively creates meaning, resulting in a whole field of textual meanngs. Textual meaning ceases to be a singular entity; rather it becomes an ongoing process of which you are a crucial part.

Now that you have been liberated to create textual meaning wherever you go (or read) it's time for thinking about how meaning can be derived from particular types of texts.

11. Unseen Poetry

What's more scary than having a monster in your house? Having an invisible monster in your house (or so they say). As we know from horror films, what's imagined is often more frightening than something seen and known. Sometimes students are trepidatious at the thought of facing an 'unseen' text, an exercise that crops up from time to time in examinations and Oxbridge interviews, most commonly using a poem.

The 'unseen' seems unsettling because it's hard to prepare for. What knowledge can you bring to the task if you've no idea about what sort of text you're going to have to analyse? Though, in essence, the 'unseen' tests skill, not retention of information, knowing something about how poems work in general and how poetry has developed over time, its major trends and fashions will help. **As ever,**  **make sure that the knowledge you use actually helps you complete the task set**. Like the little chap above, it must be useful knowledge. Even more helpful will be having a methodology and a literary toolkit, a box of tricks for unlocking even the most elliptical of poems.

The knowledge

London taxi drivers refer to 'the knowledge' as their ability to memorise roads and traffic systems. The next section of this book will provide you with the knowledge, methodology and toolkit to help you navigate the metropolis of English poetry. A very brief sketch of poetic periods should help you think in terms of the contexts of a poem. (For further information on each of the periods consult a good literary companion.)

Medieval verse was written in Middle English and is best exemplified by the work of Geoffrey Chaucer, who is sometimes referred to as 'the father of English Literature'. **Often writers of medieval verse are fond of allegory, stories, characters and social satire**. Chaucer is also celebrated for his ability to write in and subvert different literary genres, and for moving smoothly between different language registers, inter-slicing elegant courtly French and Latin phrasing with more earthy Anglo-Saxon vocabulary. Chaucer's language is often crunchily onomatopoeic and richly expressive.

In Chaucer's 'Canterbury Tales' pilgrims take it in turns to tell stories that reveal more about themselves as about their ostensible subjects. Here's the opening of Chaucer's 'General Prologue':

Whan that aprill with his shoures soote
The droghte of march hath perced to the roote,
And bathed every veyne in swich licour
Of which vertu engendred is the flour;
Whan zephirus eek with his sweete breeth
Inspired hath in every holt and heeth
Tendre croppes, and the yonge sonne
Hath in the ram his halve cours yronne,
And smale foweles maken melodye,
That slepen al the nyght with open ye

(so priketh hem nature in hir corages);
Thanne longen folk to goon on pilgrimages,
And palmeres for to seken straunge strondes,
To ferne halwes, kowthe in sondry londes;
And specially from every shires ende
Of engelond to caunterbury they wende,
The hooly blisful martir for to seke,
That hem hath holpen whan that they were seeke.

See also 'Sir Gawain and the Green Knight' and William Langland's 'Piers Plowman'.

 **Renaissance** verse was written in and around 1600. The most famous English renaissance poets are Spencer, Shakespeare, Marvell and Donne. Their language is more recognisable and more modern than Chaucer's, but the syntax can be tricky. **Elegance, boldness and wit were highly prized**. Wit could be demonstrated through dexterity with a form and through sophisticated and surprising metaphors.

Marvell and Donne are often categorised as **metaphysical poets,** a group of poets **renowned especially for their daring and original conceits**. A conceit is a comparison running throughout a poem, such as comparing your lover to a summer's day. The metaphysicals often drew their images from the emerging subject of science. Donne, for example, uses a striking image from cartography when he compares two lovers to the legs of a compass. The sonnet is a favoured form and love in all its guises is a common theme. Here's a little snippet of Shakespeare's sonnet 147:

My love is as a fever, longing still
For that which longer nurseth the disease;
Feeding on that which doth preserve the ill,
The uncertain sickly appetite to please.

See also Shakespeare's sonnets, 'The Flea' by John Donne and 'To His Coy Mistress' by Andrew Marvell.

 **The Augustans** were writing in 'The Age of Reason'. As their names suggests, their style was neoclassical, which means they drew on models from classical antiquity. The most famous poets are Alexander Pope, Samuel Johnson and John Dryden. Their poetry is the verse equivalent of elegantly proportioned Georgian country houses designed by Capability Brown.

Characterised by use of the heroic couplet, and by **emphasis on polished witty expression and on barbed social satire, Augustan poetry is also rich in reference to learned subjects, such as classical literature, contemporary religion and politics**. Augustan poets valued elevated poetic language (sometimes called 'diction') and sophistication of style. They did not bludgeon their subjects over the head with a club; their preference was for the light and elegant rapier to the guts.

Here's a short extract from Dryden's 'Absalom and Achitophel':

In pious times, ere priest-craft did begin,
Before polygamy was made a sin;
When man, on many, multipli'd his kind,
Ere one to one was cursedly confin'd:
When Nature prompted, and no Law deni'd
Promiscuous use of concubine and bride;

See also Johnson's 'On the Vanity of Human Wishes' and Pope's 'The Rape of the Lock'

The Romantics were a rebellious, politically radical bunch who rejected utterly the social themes, elevated diction and rarified aesthetics of Augustan poetry. They replaced social satire with social protest; instead of the elevated diction of the Augustans they favoured rougher, plainer, freer expression. **Their poetry focused on the communication of powerful, fervent emotion and they wanted it to change their world.** Often their subjects were ordinary people and ordinary experiences, but they were also fascinated by the mind, by childhood innocence and by human perception.

In love with wild nature, extremes of all kinds, outsiders and outcasts, dreams and visions, the Romantics used popular forms such as ballads and songs, but also rediscovered the unfashionable form of the sonnet, rebooting it for the 'age of revolutions'. Our first 'rock stars' include Byron, Shelley, Keats, Wordsworth, Blake, Coleridge and Charlotte Smith.

If Augustan poetry is like a Georgian mansion, Romantic poetry is a ruined church in the middle of a wild landscape.

For a taste of Romanticism here's the whole of Blake's 'The Sick Rose':

O Rose thou art sick.
The invisible worm,
That flies in the night
In the howling storm:
Has found out thy bed
Of crimson joy:
And his dark secret love
Does thy life destroy.

See also Wordsworth's 'Upon Westminster Bridge' and Shelley's 'Ode to the West Wind'.

Superficially **Victorian poetry** is morally earnest, sexually and stylistically

conservative. Victorian taste was certainly for well-made, well crafted poetry on serious subjects. The **power of Victorian poetry often comes, however, from what is not and cannot be said in polite society**, from the shadow of taboo subjects hinted at and alluded to through the protection of imagery. The most famous Victorian poet is Alfred Lord Tennyson. Other Victorian poets include Robert and Elizabeth (Barrett) Browning, Christina Rossetti and Gerard Manley Hopkins.

Often there is an **appeal to noble sentiments and actions couched in somewhat elegiac tones**, as if these noble qualities are rare in an increasingly industrial world. This nostalgia for a more noble, heroic age also manifests itself in a vogue for medievalism.

Perhaps overshadowed rather by the rise of the novel, Victorian poetry also typically wrestles with issues of religious faith and, towards the end of the nineteenth century, with political issues, such as environmentalism and early feminism. The aesthetics of Romanticism continue deep into the century, becoming more Gothic and introverted in Decadent writing.

Here's a flavour of Tennyson's 'Now sleeps the crimson petal':

> *Now sleeps the crimson petal, now the white;*
> *Nor waves the cypress in the palace walk;*
> *Nor winks the gold fin in the porphyry font;*
> *The firefly wakens, waken thou with me.*
> *Now droops the milk-white peacock like a ghost,*
> *And like a ghost she glimmers on to me.*
>
> *Now lies the Earth all Danae to the stars,*
> *And all thy heart lies open unto me.*
> *Now slides the silent meteor on, and leaves*

See also 'In Memoriam' by Alfred Lord Tennyson, 'Goblin Market' by Christina Rossetti and 'The Windhover' by Gerard Manley Hopkins.

Twentieth Century Modernism: another radical shift, making poetry modern again. The dusty old diction, the regular forms and grandiloquent phrasing of Victorian poetry are thrown off. Poetry needs to be modern, lean and fit, machine-like for the machine age, capable of capturing the atrocity of the first World War, advances in technology and the experience of living in modern cities. In the novel, Modernists develop the 'stream of consciousness', signalling an interest in psychology and subjective experience that Modernist poets, such as T.S. Eliot and H.D. shared.

Characterised by its difficulty and its fragmentary, non-linear structures, Modernist poetry dramatises and embodies a loss of confidence in authority. Instead of conveying a single perspective, poems become collages, moving between points of view, languages, registers, voices, tones. Conventional closed verse forms give way to free verse. **The metronome of metre is replaced with rhythms which twist and turn to fit and evoke their subject.** Meaning and language become slippery and poets write self-reflexively about the difficulty of saying exactly what they mean to say.

Modernist poets often use classical allusions ironically in order to highlight the degradations of modern life through comparison to a more heroic age. Echoing the Romantics, the poet is often presented as isolated and alienated from modern society but trapped within it.

Here's a fragment of Modernist poetry. The opening of T.S. Eliot's 'The Love

Song of J. Alfred Prufrock' is a quotation from Dante in Italian. This is followed by:

> Let us go then, you and I,
> When the evening is spread out against the sky
> Like a patient etherized upon a table;
> Let us go, through certain half-deserted streets,
> The muttering retreats
> Of restless nights in one-night cheap hotels
> And sawdust restaurants with oyster-shells:
> Streets that follow like a tedious argument
> Of insidious intent
> To lead you to an overwhelming question. . .
> Oh, do not ask, "What is it?"
> Let us go and make our visit.

See also H.D.'s 'Sea Roses' and Ezra Pound's 'The River Merchant's Wife'.

The Movement and Counter Movements: After World War Two two opposing trends emerged in English poetry. The Movement poems are characterised by their precision with the English language, their fondness for traditional English verse forms and their antipathy towards the rhetorical excesses of Romanticism and Modernism.

Typically a Movement poem's take on the world is rational, objective, calm, often ironic, sometimes sardonic, distinctly English. Distrusting fancy, inflated language and emotivism, the poet is most frequently cast as a wry, sceptical observer. The quaint absurdities, spiritual and social decay and the quiet despair of modern existence are frequent themes.

Philip Larkin is the most famous poet associated with The Movement.

Against this steady, conservative strain has kicked various forms of avant-garde postmodernism and neo-primitivism. If you're reading a poem you can pretty much understand straight away it will be influenced by The Movement aesthetics. **If what you read seems at first to be complete gobbledygook, it's probably from the more radical strain**.

Here's the start of Larkin's ironically entitled 'Essential Beauty' describing advertising hoardings.

> *In frames as large as rooms that face all ways*
> *And block the ends of streets with giant loaves,*
> *Screen graves with custard, cover slums with praise*
> *Of motor-oil and cuts of salmon, shine*
> *Perpetually these sharply-pictured groves*
> *Of how life should be. High above the gutter*
> *A silver knife sinks into golden butter,*
> *A glass of milk stands in a meadow, and*
> *Well-balanced families, in fine*
> *Midsummer weather, owe their smiles, their cars,*
> *Even their youth, to that small cube each hand*
> *Stretches towards.*

This quick jaunt through poetic history could go on for quite a while and here we must draw the line. If you want to find out more feel free to traverse the Atlantic and study the poetic habits of America. Here you will come across names like Edgar Allan Poe, Walt Whitman, Emily Dickinson, William Carlos Williams, Robert Frost, Langston Hughes, Hart Crane, e.e. cummings, Elizabeth Bishop, Robert Lowell, Sylvia Plath, Allen Ginsberg, Amiri Baraka, Charles Bukowski and many others...

Closed and open forms, free verse, regularity and irregularity

Not only is it useful to develop some awareness of the history of poetry and the work of other poets, it is helpful also to be are aware of the history of poetic forms, or at least to know what types of form to expect when writing about poetry.

The word **'closed' is used to describe poetic forms that have set rules, such as a specific number of lines or a particular metrical or rhyming pattern.** Most poetry written in English before the twentieth century was written in different types of closed form. Sonnets, limericks, haikus and villanelles are examples of closed forms. Forms which have no set number of lines are called 'open'.

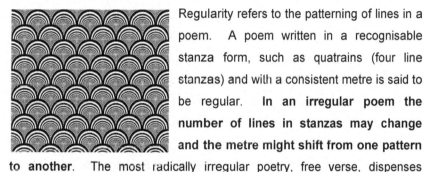

Regularity refers to the patterning of lines in a poem. A poem written in a recognisable stanza form, such as quatrains (four line stanzas) and with a consistent metre is said to be regular. **In an irregular poem the number of lines in stanzas may change and the metre might shift from one pattern to another.** The most radically irregular poetry, free verse, dispenses altogether with metre and regular stanzas. Stephen Fry in *The Ode less Travelled* quotes the American Modernist poet Ezra Pound who wrote that 'no good poetry is ever written in a manner twenty years old'. For Pound avoiding hackneyed outmodedness meant rejecting conventional diction, but also discarding popular closed and regular forms.

Indeed, some of the most radical late twentieth century poets viewed conventional poetic forms with outright hostility, believing them to be ideologically contaminated, particularly by colonialism. For American and post colonial writers, for instance, a closed form, such a sonnet, could be conceived of as a European product, pre-packaging experience to fit a closed European mindset. To a feminist poet, the same form could be conceived as essentially a male creation boxing in female experience. Rejecting conventional ways of organising words into poetry, such as number of lines, metre and rhyme scheme, radical poets sought new principles of composition. They did not wish to just copy European, male or conventional forms; they wanted to invent their own forms, reflecting their own experiences, born out of distinctly different environments. **For these radicals copying European poetic forms would have been analogous to building mock Tudor English houses on the great American plains:** foolish, muddle-headed, and backward-looking.

Similarly some poets also objected to the writer/reader relationship they saw as inherent in traditional forms such as the lyric. For these writers, the lyric privileged the supposed great wisdom of supposedly great white males. The act of reading, they believed, imposed the great writer's words and ideas on an oppressed, passive reader. Hence these poets sought a more democratic writer/reader relationship. In America, the land of the free, poets yearned for freer verse forms, poetic opened spaces suiting the vast American landscape.

The sort of liberation gained by irregular and free verse forms can come, however, at a price. **A regular form is a support system, a structural underwiring or a skeleton for a poem.** Restrictions and limits can also be helpful - all good games need rules and a poem is a sort of language game. As another American poet, Robert Frost, said, 'writing free verse is like playing tennis with the net down'. Though, perhaps, it's more like playing tennis without a court.

Certainly a poet can employ form to help express a poem's ideas or experience, or to create a tension between form and meaning. Think of a sonnet about the horrors of housework or a limerick about the suffering of a bruised heart. Form can be played with, adapted, used ironically or subverted; a form sets up a pattern. Deviations from these patterns imply points of significance. As we will suggest later when discussing narrative structure, a useful way of exploring the significance of form is to radically change it. What is the effect, for instance, of setting out the sonnet you are studying as a piece of continuous prose; what is lost or gained?

Even reclassifying a poem's form can lead to subtle shifts in meaning. For instance, Sylvia Plath's violent elegy to her father, 'Daddy' seems to express the poet's deeply ambivalent feelings towards her own dead father. However, if we read the poem as a dramatic monologue a significant gap opens up between the author and the character she has created. In this second reading we cannot so easily suppose the emotions and attitudes expressed are Plath's own.

From closed forms to free verse, we'll develop ideas about the relation of form to content in the following section on methods of analysing poems.

Tackling Poetry: The Methodology

We will suggest a number of different potential approaches, but expect you to adapt any one of them to suit your own interests. We'd recommend you try a few different methods on for size, even if the result is that you return to one you already use. Making a conscious choice about what approach you're taking means you'll be aware of the strengths and limitations of that method. If one method is not helping you analyse a poem don't be afraid to try a different one. **The key is to be flexible, adapting your approach to the suit the text you're examining**.

So, what method do you currently use to analyse a poem and where did you learn this? Is this approach something you've deliberately developed or been taught, or have you just picked it up as you've gone along? In the introduction we mentioned being given a rather cumbersome mnemonic TOC KF VPIF MRSEAR, or something like that. As we said then, the problem with this is the randomness of the terms. We prefer the toolkit idea rather than the checklist.

You might be tempted to write about a poem line by line, stanza by stanza, working on the theory that following the structure of the poem will be helpful. There's only one problem with this theory - it's a really bad one. Though we won't recommend a specific approach, we will tell you categorically what not to do: **under no circumstances whatsoever should you adopt a chronological or sequential approach to analysing a poem**!

A chronological approach is organised in the same order as the poem itself. Paragraphs typically start with 'In the first line / stanza of the poem...' and continue in subsequent paragraphs with 'in the second / third / fourth, nth paragraph'. What's wrong with this simple approach? We've already mentioned some of this earlier, but it's so important it's worth re-emphasising, we think.

- Firstly your essay should advance an interpretation of the poem. **Each paragraph should be connected by the central thread of your thesis or argument**, as we said earlier like the words running through a stick of rock. Your essay's structure should be dictated by the logic of your argument. You cannot do this if your essay's structure follows that of the poem.

- Secondly such an approach is likely to lead to lots of clumsy repetition. If the poet uses a striking image of love in the first and fourth stanzas or a similar sonic effect at different points in the poem **it would be more effective to discuss these examples together, to cross-reference**. Such an approach demonstrates that you understand poetry works like music as a network of interconnected parts.

- Thirdly **a chronological approach encourages students to describe or summarise the content or narrative in the poem**. Just as narrative summary is worth little in essays on prose, it will be rewarded few marks if any on an 'unseen' poetry task.

- Finally, students following this approach **tend to write about the first few stanzas in detail and then, as they begin to run out of time, about the last few stanzas in less detail**. This also means they can find it hard to write about the shape and structure of a poem, such as how its ending relates to its opening.

An example, as ever, should help. We'll use Blake's 'The Sick Rose' because we've just quoted it, it's short and it's a great poem.

Compare the following two sample responses.

1. In the opening line of Blake's poem he addresses the rose which he describes, surprisingly, as being 'sick' - an example of personification. Blake switches his focus in the next lines to the 'worm' which he also describes in an unusual way. Firstly it is 'invisible' (so how does he know it's there?) and secondly it's flying in a storm. The fact that the storm is 'howling' in the stanzas last line is also significant, perhaps suggesting either despair or predatory violence.

In the second stanza the worm seems to have discovered a bed, which we assume to be the rose's with the idea of flower / marriage bed. So the poem is still being addressed to the rose. The rose's bed is described as being 'crimson' and the love the worm feels for the rose is described as 'dark, secret'. In the stanza's last line this love results in the destruction of the rose, 'thy life destroyed'.

So, what do you think of this? It's not utterly contemptible drivel, is it? It isn't all summary of the narrative, and in this case, the narrative is actually pretty interesting. There is some engagement with the language too and the devices Blake uses. Notice too the sense of the effect of the poem as the reader tries to decipher its symbolism.

But even in this short example **you should be able to see how repetitive and mechanical this essay would be if it were dealing with a longer poem**. By the 'in the third stanza...' the approach will begin to pall. Moreover what point is served by the references to where the lines occur, such as 'in the opening line'? If this information is significant in terms of the poem's structure then the candidate should comment on it. And wouldn't it be useful to make some links between the words and images across the two stanzas? Consider an alternative approach:

> *2. Blake's poem explores what the poet considers to be the deadly effects of secret, selfish love. The phallic masculine image of the worm attacks and destroys the feminine rose, either because his love is illicit, itself a form of corruption, hence its secrecy, or perhaps as a punishment for the rose's self-indulgence in her crimson bed which has excluded the worm. Either way, Blake creates a claustrophobically vivid, sexually charged, almost riddle-like narrative. Through his use of colour and nature symbolism combined with the pressure he exerts on form Blake generates an unsettling intense effect.*

How is this second example different? Firstly it focuses on ideas, what the candidate takes to be the poem's central concern. Having explained this briefly, they go on to discuss the overall effect, with some indication of the methods used to achieve this. Overall this is a promising start...

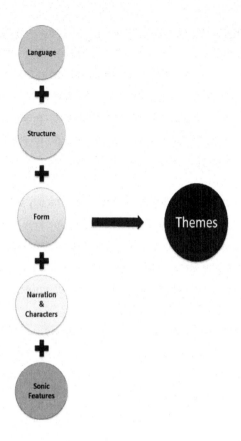

A glittering array of methods

So now that you know not to follow the chronological road, what do we actually want you to do? What follows is an outline of multiple approaches to unlocking poetic meaning. Try one, try some, try them all if you wish, but remain open-minded at all times. Remember though that reading a poem is not merely an intellectual exercise: It is also like listening to a piece of music or looking at a painting. Writing about the aesthetic impact of the words, the experience of reading them *on you* is also a vital part of a high level response.

Whichever of the following methods you use, the key thing is that to come up with a reading of the poem which is convincing to your reader.

1. Pick out the most interesting features and comment on them

Historically poems were often judged by the number of great lines they contained. Great lines were the ones which stuck in the reader's mind after just a couple of readings. Originally poetry was an oral art form; images, rhymes, rhythm were devices to help the orator remember the poem for oral recital. Usually the most memorable language has some metaphorical originality, some strikingly visual or sonic effect.

The tradition of focusing specifically on the poet's facility with metaphor can be traced back (like so many literary subjects) to Aristotle's 'Poetics':

> *'...the greatest thing by far is to have a command of metaphor. This alone cannot be imparted by another; it is the mark of genius – for to make good metaphors implies an eye for resemblances'.*

Professor Terry Eagleton, in his book *How to Read a Poem*, makes a more general point about poetic language:

> *'poetry exploits the resources of language more intensely than most of our everyday speech'.*

To do this poets often disrupt normal patterns of language, combining words in unusual ways.

A useful term here is 'collocation', a word employed by linguists to describe the way some words tend to fit naturally together. A few examples of collocation: 'fish and' is often connected to 'chips'; if something is very 'clear' it is frequently described as 'crystal clear'; the noise of sausages cooking is usually described as 'sizzling'. Poetry often works by breaking these habitual patterns of language, or collocation. The name of a famous pop group illustrates the idea: 'The Artic Monkeys' is a memorable name because of the combination of contrary words - they don't 'compute'. 'The Sizzling Walruses' would also have worked quite well... perhaps.

Pulling out and examining the most interesting lines, phrases and techniques has the merit of allowing you to focus on the bits of the texts you'll have most to write about. What are the disadvantages of this approach? For one thing, it's not very systematic or objective. It doesn't encourage you to see the poem as a whole as it focuses attention on just a few isolated lines. It would be like concentrating only on the trees in the visual above without considering the lake or failing to put them into the context of the wider visual of object and reflection. This approach also makes it hard to discuss how various aspects of the poem interrelate and contribute the overall impact of a poem. Another problem is what to do if you're faced with a poem that doesn't use fancy 'poetic language' or obviously highly wrought poetic devices.

2. A stylistics approach

This method is the opposite of the one above. It derives from critics who wanted to make the analysis of poetry less like the appreciation of art and more like a science (see chapter 19 for our discussion of structuralism). Hence the method is more systematic, seemingly less subjective and more focused on the whole text (or to continue the science references) the whole data set.

Stylistic analysis breaks the text down grammatically and then examines each part. So, for example we could extract the nouns from Blake's poem, explore these, and then move on to the verbs, adjectives, pronouns, prepositions and conjunctions. If this sounds too arid, give it a try. It's often surprisingly useful, forcing the reader to make connections across a text; for instance, gathering all the adjectives together for closer inspection to see what they reveal.

Examination of the verbs in Blake's poem reveals something rather curious. That first verb 'art' is in the present tense. So the poet is addressing a living rose. The present tense continues with 'flies'. We might expect, therefore, that the following verb to be in the future tense, 'will find out'. Instead it's in the past, 'has found out'. Again we might assume a future tense would follow. Instead Blake finishes in the present, 'does'. What is the effect of this time-bending structure? We'll leave that for you to ponder. Hopefully though, even this brief example illustrates the potential of foregrounding particular aspects of grammar.

Of course, grammar also includes syntax (word order, or how words touch each other) as well as sentence type and function. A stylistic analysis of a poem would also include inspection of the poem's sonic features.

In the diagram below, we have separated out the various nouns, verbs, adjectives and pronouns into separate boxes. (The word 'O' is grammatically an interjection, though the literary term for this is an apostrophe.)

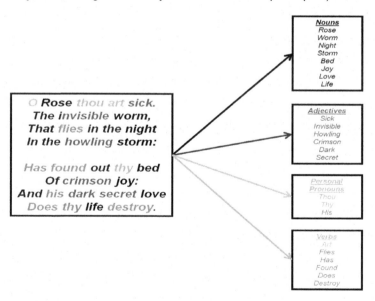

Coding the poem grammatically might help us to notice how all the nouns are monosyllables of Anglo-Saxon origin and that the more complex words are the adjectives. Obviously this is just the first step towards analysis, but it's an interesting pattern.

3. Lexical and semantic fields

Another approach drawn from linguistic analysis focuses on lexical and semantic fields. Lexis is another word for vocabulary. Lexical fields refer to types of language associated with particular ideas, activities, subjects. So in the lexical field associated with football are words like 'goalkeeper', 'tackle', 'header' as well as phrases such as 'at the end of the day' and 'a game of two halves'. The lexical field for literary study, in contrast, would include words such as 'narrative', 'metaphor' and 'poem'. All texts are constructed from language used elsewhere at other times in other contexts, from different lexical fields. Combinations of different lexical fields generate linguistic texture.

Lexis can also refer to different categories of language. Groups of words that come from Old English or those that derive from modern technology are sometimes called lexical layers. In Blake's poem for instance the pronouns ('thou' and 'thy') are deliberately archaic, whereas his verb forms are modern, such as 'flies' rather than 'flieth'.

Semantics is closely related to lexis. **A semantic field refers to words connected in meanings**. So there is a semantic field of words to do with love, or jealousy, for example. One, unusual and useful way of seeing a poem is as a collision of different lexical and semantic fields. Like the focus on grammar, one huge benefit of this approach is that it makes the reader focus on connections and patterns of meaning. Over the page is an example of the sort of lexico-semantic fields to be found in Blake's poem:

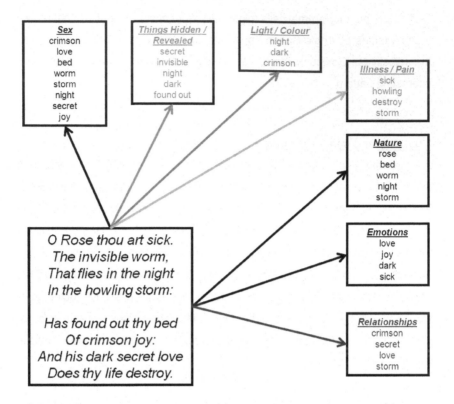

Sex	Things Hidden / Revealed	Light / Colour
crimson	secret	night
love	invisible	dark
bed	night	crimson
worm	dark	
storm	found out	
night		
secret		
joy		

Illness / Pain
sick
howling
destroy
storm

Nature
rose
bed
worm
night
storm

Emotions
love
joy
dark
sick

Relationships
crimson
secret
love
storm

O Rose thou art sick.
The invisible worm,
That flies in the night
In the howling storm:

Has found out thy bed
Of crimson joy:
And his dark secret love
Does thy life destroy.

4. A literary approach

If the last two approaches seem a little dry, even unpoetic to you, you might prefer a more literary approach. Poetry, after all, is literary and often employs highly descriptive, musical and patterned language. As we've noted previously, the term 'diction' refers to the sort of literary language thought traditionally to be fitting and appropriate for poetry. The diction of a Romantic poet would, for example, be very different to that of an Augustan, or a Modernist.

It seems sensible, therefore, to focus primarily on a poem's diction, its imagery, sonic qualities and its poetic form. **In particular poets tend to use heightened language as well as figurative and sensory imagery**. Symbolism refers to use of established metaphorical images, such as a white dove of peace or the colour red symbolising passion and danger. Imagery is more individual and idiosyncratic.

What would you do if confronted with a poem devoid of obvious poetic techniques, written in perfectly ordinary everyday language? What seems poetic language to one generation of writers and readers comes to be seen as outmoded, inflated and contrived to succeeding generations. Modern poets, in particular, favour everyday language, tending to eschew poetic flourishes and heightened, special diction. So, once again, you'll need to be able to adapt your method to suit the text.

Used well, the four approaches outlined above are more than sufficient to achieve a high grade in English A-level. If you're happy with these, skip the next short section. On the other hand, if you want to push yourself further, you're doing a degree in English or you're just interested in different approaches, here are a few more to consider.

5. 'Space made Articulate': Looking to modern art...

In his very useful book on modern poetry, *Contemporary poetry*, Ian Brinton uses the analogy of Japanese gardens and the occasional drip of their bamboo water features. The drip is not to draw attention to itself. Rather it is to make us hear the silence that surrounds it. Or think of the importance of the gaps between notes, Brinton suggests, in a piece of music. He quotes the poet Charles Tomlinson's observation that, 'Reality is to be sought, not in concrete/ But in space made articulate'.

Conventionally, plays are about things that happen, about action. In Beckett's *Waiting for Godot* he inverts the conventional pattern by making waiting for something to happen the central 'action' of his tragic-comedy. Right, we're sure you've got the idea.

You may have spotted here a connection to what we said earlier about answering a question by coming at it from an unusual angle, through the back door, and to the idea of examining a text through the prism of a minor character. This is indeed similar thinking. How though can we apply this to our analysis of poetry?

We'd need to look past the showy bits of language in a poem to focus instead on the function words which provide the supporting structure. We'd also notice the underpinning structure of syntax and how the lines of the poem are shaped in space. We might also **focus on the gaps in the poem, its unstressed beats or the bits of the story left out**. Whether this approach would prove fruitful on 'The Sick Rose' would only become evident through its application.

6. Semiotics

The term 'semiotics' refers to the study of language as a system of signs. Semioticians break words and phrases, or signs, down into **signifiers** and **signified**, the latter of which can change depending on the context in which the signifier is used. The signifier 'red light', for instance, has a different signified (or meaning) when found on the top of a police car than when it's located in a dubious area of a city. Misunderstanding this signifier could get you into trouble.

The ideas of semiotics can be applied to any aspect of culture, including literature. For example, **the Russian semiotician Yuri Lotman argues that a poem is not just a system of interconnected signs, but a 'system of systems'**. By this he means that each of the separate components of a poem, its metre, imagery, form, rhyme scheme and so forth, operates within a separate system. These systems interact with each other, sometimes working together, sometimes pulling in different directions. A poet could, for instance, create an interesting effect if they used a jaunty metrical system for a poem about mourning.

So a word, phrase or image from a poem will be part of the poem's semantic system, how it makes meaning, but it will also be part of its sound system, as well as its rhythmical system. Traditionally poetry is seen as an art form in which the various aspects - imagery, rhythm, form and so forth - work harmoniously together to create an integrated whole. For Lotman, however, **it is the friction of the different systems rubbing against each other that creates interesting poetic effects**.

If we take the opening line from Seamus Heaney's poem, 'Churning Day' we should be able to apply Lotman's ideas.

'A thick-crust, coarse-grained as limestone rough-cast'.

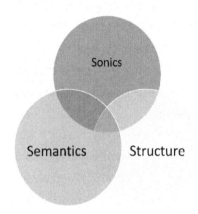

Three systems can be seen to be operating here. Firstly the poem's metrical system, its structural underwiring, is iambic tetrameter.

'A **thick**-crust, **coarse**-grained as **lime**stone **rough**-cast'

However the poem's sonic system disrupts this pattern. Notice, for example, how the alliteration of 'crust', 'coarse', 'cast' is reinforced by the similar sounds of the 'crust' and 'coarse' and by the consonance of 'crust' and 'cast'. Add to this the assonance linking 'crust' to 'rough' and the harsh 'k' and sibilant 's' sounds. The sonic system links and gives stress to words that should be unstressed in the metrical system.

In the poem's third system, its semantic one, the words that fall in the downbeats - 'crust', 'grained', 'stone' and 'cast' - also carry significant meaning. Compare the line, for instance, with another line of iambic tetrameter - 'He walks along the winding road'. In the second example the unstressed downbeats clearly fall on words and sounds that are merely functional - 'he', 'a', 'the', 'ing'.

In Heaney's line, in contrast, the sonic and semantic systems are working together. And both are, in Lotman's terms, in conflict with the metrical system. The effect of these different systems operating with and against each other is to thicken the line to match the physicality of the material described.

7. Theoretical approaches

Our last approach is more overtly theoretical. The approaches outlined above may not have been overtly theoretical with a capital T, but nevertheless they all reveal particular values, biases and aesthetic judgements about literature and writing about literature. All of the above could, for instance, be called formalist approaches or intrinsic approaches. Whether they wear their critical heart on their sleeve or whether their theoretical assumptions are implicit, tno approach isn't theoretical in some sense. If theoretical approaches are your thing, you may want to jump forward to chapter 19.

Why bother to use a theoretical approach? Well, **each theoretical approach asks different questions about a text**. So explicitly theoretical approaches might be productive with Blake's poem because their questions open up new paths for further exploration. A feminist reading, for instance, would reveal interesting things to interrogate about how notions of masculinity and femininity are constructed in the text. Another useful approach to the analysis of any text is drawn from Structuralism. According to Structuralist critics all texts are organised through the relationships of binary opposites, such as up/down, dead/alive, black/white. Examination of these binary opposites reveals the underpinning structure of ideas in a text. A Historicist reading would explore how Blake's themes of corrupt beauty, deceptive appearances and jealous love relate to the revolutionary world in which the poet lived and worked.

Further Thoughts - syntax and texture, rhythm and metre

As we've seen, the arrangement of words, phrases and clauses in a sentence is called 'syntax'. The critic Timothy Morton suggests a useful way of thinking about syntax is in terms of heat: **'Hot syntax' can be used to refer to densely packed language; 'cold syntax' to language that is more loosely constructed.** As evinced by our own spatial metaphors, syntax can also be written about in terms of looseness and tightness, density and spareness.

In Morton's terms, the line we quoted earlier from Seamus Heaney's poem 'Churning Day' would be 'hot' because the important, meaning-carrying words are bunched up so closely together. Indeed only two words in the line, 'a' and 'as' would clearly be unstressed:

> '<u>A</u> thick-crust, coarse-grained <u>as</u>
> limestone rough-cast'

Sometimes critics write about the texture of a poem. It should be clear from reading Heaney's line that he creates a thick, rough texture to the first sentence of his poem. Texture is created by the interplay of different aspects of the language, such as the syntax, the rhythm and the sound qualities of the words individually as well as the way they rub together. What could we say about the texture of Blake's poem? Certainly it's much harder to identify in this instance, for one thing. Texture is a term that can be kept tucked away in the toolkit, ready to use only on a suitably rough or smooth poem.

What's the difference between the closely related words 'metre' and 'rhythm'? Is 'metre' fixed and objective, whereas rhythm is interpretable? Metre refers to the stress pattern of poem. If the poem is in a closed form then this stress pattern will remain the same throughout the poem. Rhythm is created by the interaction between a stress pattern, such as iambic pentameter, with other elements of the poem's language such as the sounds of the words and the syntax. Lee Spinks provides a particularly clear distinction between the two words in *The Edinburgh Introduction to Studying English*:

> '*By metre, I mean the definitive patterned stress-shape of a poem (the way its beats are organised into a coherent and repeatable form such as iambic pentameter or trochaic verse), while by rhythm I mean the sound or shapes that this metrical pattern creates as the poem unfolds during the time of our reading..*'

The iambic tetrameter, for instance, is a metre often associated with song like poems. Yet in the opening line of 'Churning Day' this metre is slowed and weighed down by the density of interactions between the sounds of the words and by the 'hot', dense syntax.

Conclusion

Try out a few different approaches. Don't get stuck using the same one all the time. Some poems will reveal more if you apply a stylistics approach. Others may require a gendered reading. It really does depend on the poem. The key is to have a range of approaches at your fingertips and the flexibility to try different ones at different times. Thus these various methods are in themselves different literary toolkits, offering you a whole range of instruments to help unpick a poem.

Fundamentally you'll always need to write about a few key features of poems that make them poems (and not songs or novels, or oranges). Ultimately, for any unseen poem we'd recommend employing the appropriate tools; whatever method you adopt, ensure that you analyse:

- The aesthetic and emotional impact the poem has on you / the reader.
- The themes of the poem or the experience it evokes
- The language: especially figurative & sensory imagery, but also the types of words used, even the seemingly less important ones, as well as any unusual combinations of words / phrases. Does the poem employ 'poetic language'? Where else might you find this language? Can you recognise words from specific lexical fields?
- The sound qualities: Poetry is the closest words come to music. Part of the aesthetic impact, the sonic qualities of poems are at least as important as the 'meaning'. Consider rhyme, half rhyme, assonance, alliteration, rhythm, onomatopoeic effects. (For a really useful book on sound in poetry look up *52 Ways of Looking at a Poem* by Ruth Padel).

- The formal and structural features: This should include examining whether the poem is regular or irregular, closed or open form. Different types of poems, such as sonnets, dramatic monologues, free verse and lyrics work in different ways, so you need to explore how the poet employs the form and whether they subvert its conventions. Look for breaks or deviations in patterns - these are often significant. Consider too aspects such as metre, stanza form, lineation, enjambment and caesuras as well as rhyme schemes.
- Put the pieces back together: Having dismantled a poem's precision engineering, explore how its various components, such as how the language and the form, work in relation to each other.

Now that we've equipped you with the necessary tools, please use them. You'll need them.

12. A Poem in the Light of Others by the Same Poet

Some exam boards set this sort of task. Usually you will be given a poem from a collection you've studied in class and be asked to analyse it in the context of this study. In these tasks the context of the other poems is your first and most important context and you will, therefore, have to make explicit reference to the other poems.

To reach the highest marks **the trick is to try to develop an overview of the poet's primary concerns, stylistic traits and formal preferences**. It also helps if you can place his or her writing within a tradition he or she is working within or against. Some poets have long writing careers and most of us change considerably from when we are young to when we are old. Therefore **it's helpful to have a sense of the chronology of the poems and the development of the poet's work over time**.

 For example if you're studying the work of W.B. Yeats it's productive to think of his poetry as developing in three broad stages. Yeats's early poetry is sonorous, late-Romantic dreamy escapism, with an Irish mythological twist. His middle period poetry is characterised by greater political focus on the contemporary world. His late poetry can be defined by its uneasy relation to the fragmentary aesthetics of Modernism.

As you read more Yeats poems and more criticism, you'll realise that this tripartite division of his work doesn't quite hold. Though his poetry does certainly develop, there are continuities in style and ideas throughout his oeuvre. But the tripartite categorisation is a useful starting point, a way of loosely grouping the poems, looking at what they have in common and what separates them.

The student who can write about how a particular feature, such as an image, rhythmical quirk or a turn of phrase is unusual in the work of the poet, or who can comment on how a particular motif develops in a poet's work is a superior student.

To develop this superior overview, think of the poems as a text, as a whole, like a novel. Seen in this light what story do they tell about the poet and his or her concerns? **Try to group the poems under as many different headings as you can**. Arrange them thematically, stylistically, in terms of form. Arrange them in chronological order, in the order of which ones you like best to least. Arrange by what pieces of music they're most like. Use pie charts, Venn diagrams, flow diagrams to help you visualise the connections.

When revising use critics and different theoretical perspectives to open new territory. For example, what would postcolonial or feminist critics have to say about Yeats's work?

13. Collections of Poems

The same preparation will really help you to write authoritatively about a collection of poems. But how do you organise your writing on a collection? A common approach is to pick a few exemplar poems and to work through these in a sequence, stopping to analyse each one in turn. Commonly on Seamus Heaney's *Death of a Naturalist* students write about the titular poem, 'Digging', 'Follower' and a couple more. On Blake's poetry poems like 'London', 'The Tyger', 'Holy Thursday' and 'Nurse's Song' come up a lot and are often explored as separate units of meaning.

Though this approach can be successful, there's the same danger of clunky repetition as there was in taking a sequential approach to a single poem. As we suggested earlier, think of the poems as a single text and you will be able to see the potential problem more clearly. In particular, take this poem-by-poem approach and it will be hard to explore patterns across the text and to cross-reference effectively. **A better technique then is to focus on key aspects of the poems as a group**. Then you can write about these key features, **such as motifs (repeated patterns of language) and themes (repeated patterns of ideas) ranging across the collection as a whole**. At some stage you may want to stop and focus on a specific poem that best exemplifies your point, so that you have both breadth and depth.

Characteristically the Romantics thought of a poem as organic. In contrast, the Modernists conceived of a poem as being like a machine, a machine made to remember itself. Your job is to dissect the organism or disassemble the machine, to examine more closely its constituent parts. Put the parts of the poem and the collection of poems under the microscope. It's like taking the back off a watch to examine the cogs and wheels of imagery, or to open a car's bonnet to explore the engine of metre.

Just as context helps to explain text, to understand how the organism lives or the machine works, you'll also need to put it back together again. Otherwise you won't be able to see how the parts work together to make the thing breathe and go.

The essential point is that a great poem and a great poetry collection should be an integrated system, lithe and efficient. Any word, image, beat that isn't contributing should have been cut. Therefore each part of the apparatus of poetry is worth your close inspection.

As with the focus on incidental characters in Shakespeare and the function words and syntax in poetry, **we recommend you try to deviate from the very familiar and often used poems by major poets**. Firstly, it's hard to say much that is new about these poems; secondly the examiners will have read many essays on these poems; thirdly using less familiar poems allows you to show you can apply critics' observations to new contexts.

For example, very few A-level students write about Blake's lesser known poems in the *Songs of Innocence and Experience*. Only the very boldest explore the esoteric *Prophetic Books* or *The Book of Thel*. Really useful and fascinating extracts from these books are included in the cheap everyman edition of Blake's poems. Similarly with Heaney an essay that focused on the poems in *Death of a Naturalist* he excluded from his Selected Poems would be fresh and interesting. A cursory look at Plath's selected poems reveals poems such as 'The Hermit at the Outermost House' that are very rarely written about.

You might take this further and say why study the most famous, most written about poets. What about great, less famous poets? If you want to study Romantic poetry, for example, how about reading Charlotte Smith? There's a balance to be struck here between following the mainstream of literature, covering some of the big beasts, and going off on tributaries to explore less navigated territory where many strange and brilliant creatures lurk; which leads us nicely onto the brilliant lurking creature that is prose writing.

14. Writing about Prose Fiction: The Novel and the Short Story

As with all things literary, no matter what type of question you answer the central thing for you to understand will be the relationship between the ideas explored and the various strategies used to help explore these ideas. **The prose writer, like the poet and the dramatist, has a number of narrative tools at their disposal and they will use them as they see fit to get their message across.** Your job is to identify which tools are used and what role they play in eliciting a response from the reader and ultimately how all these combine to provide textual meaning. To further complicate things at A-Level and beyond, the impact of context and critical reception on meaning will start to play a more active role. We will identify and discuss these new intruders later on.

This section follows the predominance of the novel in literature in recent times but will digress to the short story where appropriate. We do not intend to enter the debate about what constitutes a novel, how it differs from a novella and certainly not how a novel is not a short story and vice versa. These are discussions for another forum. Suffice to say we will assume that you will know what a novel is, or at least that your teacher has told you that the bundle of pages you intend to write about is a novel. If you remember them calling it a short story then skip to the section on form for more details.

So back to the novel. Compared to poetry, it is a relatively new literary form - a child of the 18th century. However, in its short literary life it has displaced poetry as the main vehicle for literary travel. A quick survey of any decent bookshop will confirm this. Like their poetic brethren prose writers have an array of different strategies that they can employ at an intratextual level (**within** the text itself). However, you as a student must also be aware of intertextual considerations, such as form, genre and mode, where you can describe the relationships **between** different literary texts.

The diagrams below illustrate the different things you must reflect upon before embarking on writing your essay about any prose text.

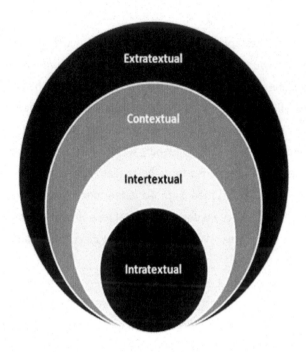

Intratextual: narrator and narrative perspective; narrative structure [overall trajectory vs. specific story packaging]; language and style; settings; characterisation; all elements that produce the theme/message of the text

Intertextual: mode; genre; form

Contextual: author's biography; period of production [socio-historical/cultural]; literary context/artistic movement

Extratextual: critical reception [at moment of production and thereafter]

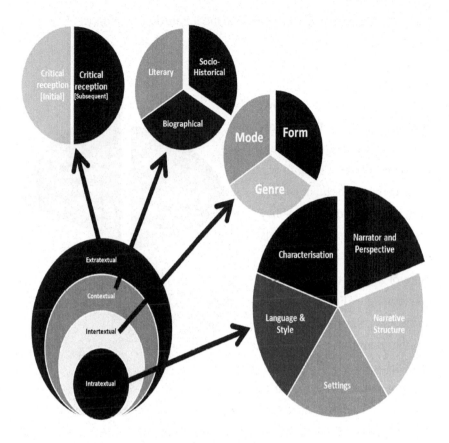

In this section, we will consider the first two layers; the intratextual and intertextual. More than likely your essay question will not be "discuss the effectiveness of the various intratextual and intertextual factors that contribute to meaning in X's novel Z." However, if you have a deep understanding of these factors the quality of your discussion will be markedly improved as you swoop in and out of the text perching at the various textual levels to validate your points. A useful way of thinking about analysing prose is to compare it with the previous section on analysing poetry. Writing about prose must be based on intense, close readings of the text; like a series of connected poems. Obviously, you will not have the space to do this for an entire novel as it would go on for quite a long time. However, you should be looking for key episodes related to your essay topic and subjecting them to detailed analysis. This will ensure that the foundations for your analysis are deeply rooted in the text as well as allowing you to excavate interesting aspects not immediately obvious. So firstly down to the intratextual boundary.

Intratextual Factors

The following narrative strategies are the most commonly used and will vary from text to text. It is up to you to ascertain which ones are most relevant and also how they are relevant to your essay. It is certainly not an exhaustive list; more of a quick checklist to get you started. For reasons of space, we have concentrated on the narrative aspects that students usually should explore in more detail in their essays.

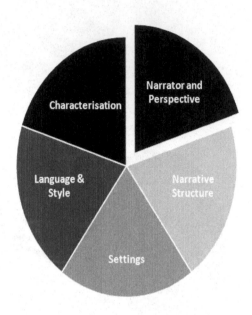

We do not intend to describe how to write about theme or setting in this section. That should already be well grounded from GCSE. AS English study requires more analytical sophistication than GCSE so taking a new microscope and applying it to familiar things can be very useful. In this section, the role of narrators, language and style, characterisation and narrative structure will be examined in some detail. For further information on the narrative strategies available to prose writers we suggest reading David Lodge's informative and highly readable *The Art of Fiction*. Students often incorrectly categorise *theme* as a narrative device; it isn't. The themes that the author explores are produced by the narrative devices employed.

Narrators

The most obvious place to start is with the choice of narrator; essentially the storyteller. "But hold it - isn't the author telling the story?" you rightly exclaim. By now, hopefully, you will realise that the author and narrator are not the same entity, even though this can be difficult to discern. It is one of the most fundamental choices that must be made by an author and your first job is to ascertain who is telling the story, why the author has chosen this narrator and most importantly how this choice contributes to textual meaning. There is a number of different options:

- Narrator who participates in the story: This is a first person narrator who sometimes can be called by the intimidating moniker of homodiegetic narrator. Such narrators can be a major character directly involved in the action like Alex in *A Clockwork Orange* or be more of a minor character who observes the main action from the periphery, like Lockwood in *Wuthering Heights*. There is also the possibility of a combination of both, involved yet marginalised. A perfect example is *The Great Gatsby*'s Nick Carraway.

- Narrator who does not participate in the story: This is the third person narrator, who also goes under the much grander title of heterodiegetic narrator. Again there are various options. There is the all-knowing, omniscient narrator who can see into any character they choose and seems to be a wise guide through the story. Such narrators are typical of most Victorian literature; see George Eliot's *Middlemarch* for example. This omniscience can be tampered with by playing around with the point of view or the access to characters' thoughts. A limited or restricted third person narrator only sees the story from the point of view on one character, major or minor; see Katherine Mansfield's Leila in *Her First Ball*. An objective third person narrator remains external to all characters; a narrator who acts more like a video camera in a documentary. These are a rarity.

These various narrators can also be impartial (remaining emotionally distant from the story and characters) or partial (where they sway the reader's response to characters and events through their presentation). Again, Nick Carraway would be a classic partial narrator as he elevates bootlegger Jay Gatsby into a beautiful fertile symbol of the American Dream. To help navigate your way through this jungle of narration, **you should consider**

each type and think about the advantages and disadvantages of each one. When thinking about the specific narrator(s) of your chosen text it is quite useful to imagine how changing the narrator would change the overall effect. What would happen to Mary Shelley's *Frankenstein* if the competing first person narrators were shed and an impartial omniscient one was used instead?

To further complicate considerations of narrator, **if they are homodiegetic, we must consider them as characters in their own right**. This necessitates a consideration of narrative voice. What does your storyteller sound like? Educated, effusive and 'honest' like Nick Carraway? Scottish and working class like Renton in *Trainspotting*? Egotistical and self-promoting, like Victor Frankenstein? A consideration of this aspect of a narrator usually leads to interesting portals deeper into the text. If Frankenstein is the hero of his own novel does his hysterical voice begin to grate on the nerves and subtly reduce his notions of heroic grandeur? Do his constant high emotional states reinforce or undermine his credibility as a man of reason and science? The subtleties of such analysis will enrich your essay writing no end as they will reveal tensions and discrepancies not immediately obvious at first glance.

Characterisation

Naturally this leads us to characterisation itself. What is it and why is it so important? Obviously, it's all to do with character and you should be familiar with character study type questions from your GCSE studies. Like looking at a text at various levels, **characterisation also needs to be understood as a multilayered narrative strategy**. Before we look at these levels it must be said that characters in prose texts are fictional, they are not real people; and so you should not talk about them as if they are. Some students can make up whole psychologies based on imaginative speculation. This can be fruitful [especially if considering Freudian repressed desires etc] but can be dangerously digressive too. **You must be sensible: work with the textual evidence**. If your character based point seems flimsy, it probably is and needs to be omitted, no matter how interesting.

Sci-Fi fans will be well aware of *The Matrix* film with Keanu Reeves. In it there is a scene where he can finally see the Matrix, the virtual world his mind sees, for what is actually is: a huge computer code. This scene shows a world full of moving code but recognisable shapes. One of these shapes is a walking, talking agent made completely of numbers and letters out to annihilate our hero. Well, characterisation is not much different - it is another virtual creation only using words rather than computer code.

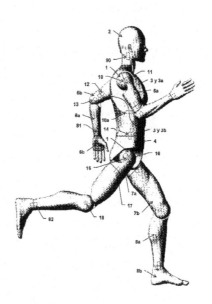

Characters are not real. They may appear real due to the cunning use of words by an author and your active imagination; which is how you might describe the most basic step of successful characterisation. They appear to be real. And this is where you begin. Like the Matrix, you must look to the most basic level and examine the key building blocks of characterisation. What words are used by the author to conjure up the physicality of a character?

Most people remember that Lennie is the big one and George the small one from Steinbeck's *Of Mice and Men*. However, looking carefully at its opening, the novel brings our attention to how George "was small and quick, dark of face, with restless eyes and sharp, strong features." In complete contrast, Lennie is described as "a huge man, shapeless of face [...] dragging his feet a little, the way a bear drags his paws." Steinbeck provides us with one of the most condensed examples of characterisation you are likely to find: the odd coupling, George's restless intelligence and awareness of life's harshness, Lennie's slow mind but potentially dangerous animal anger. Compare this to the physicality of Jay Gatsby, a character notoriously vague and hard to pin down: "there was something gorgeous about him." But what was it that was so gorgeous? The only memorable physical detail provided is his characteristic; the one "with a quality of life-affirming reassurance in it." This vagueness of physical detail has something to do with allowing Gatsby to embody the American Dream, a vague concept, rather like Gatsby himself.

This level of characterisation is the most fundamental and probably the easiest one to identify. All the things that allow us to imagine the way a character looks, walks, talks and acts may be described as **explicit characterisation**, in that they are details that are made obvious to the reader and need to be made obvious. This will also apply to how the actions of a character are viewed by other characters. Such information is put there to guide our sympathies and will affect us in a more subtle way even if it is still explicitly described by the author. For example, how does Walton's response to Frankenstein guide reader response at the end of *Frankenstein*? By this stage, the reader has access to both Victor and the creature's competing narrative accounts so our sympathies may lie in the balance. However, what are we to think when Walton describes the "untimely extinction of this glorious spirit" (Frankenstein) who is visited by a creature of "such loathsome, yet appalling hideousness"? It is pretty clear on one level. However, the complexity of characterisation employed by Shelley allows us to question such blatant favouritism. Walton's obvious affections for Frankenstein make him too unreliable a judge and the reader is left to fend for themselves.

Surveying the various **relationships between characters can be an interesting and fertile exercise**. A fun but useful way of thinking about character compatibilities is to imagine different characters going for a summer picnic. Which groupings will be harmonious and which ones will be tense, awkward affairs? Why would this happen? "Cucumber sandwich, abhorred fiend that thou art!?" Victor Frankenstein might say to his beloved offspring. What does it tell us about the different characters and their relative importance in the larger scheme of the novel? Another useful method is to construct **proximity diagrams for main characters** (basically concentric circles around a character that represent the closeness of that character to other characters) visually capture relationships between characters and also how these can change over the course of the novel. Looking at *Frankenstein*, Victor begins surrounded by a loving, if slightly suffocating, family then isolates himself through his increasingly obsessive scientific experimentation before becoming entwined in the lethal relationship with his offspring. What is Shelley trying to say about social relationships through this character journey? The context of the misunderstood Romantic genius is presented in a poor light when viewed through this prism of character relationships.

Hovering above the text surveying character relationships leads nicely to considering what **function or role a character plays in a text.** Both Lennie from *Of Mice and Men* and Frankenstein's creature are agents of chaos in their respective texts; irreparably damaging the fabric of their narrative worlds and forcing transformative situations upon other characters. Nick Carraway and Walton play similar roles too: both are self-interested, supposedly objective observers the reader must depend upon to be honest. Some chance! Their role is that of chronicler, recording an important story that captures a specific zeitgeist, but also that of judge, assessing the moral worth of the central 'hero'. Carraway's withholding of specific physical description of Gatsby (except that sensational smile) universalises Gatsby in a way that allows Gatsby to symbolise the American Dream. Gatsby's almost physical blankness allows him to become more alive to readers as they imaginatively partake in his creation. It is obvious that our

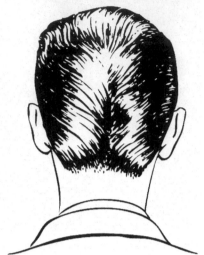

exploration of character is beginning to climb out of the text and move into the realms of **implicit characterisation**. The author does not tell the reader explicitly that Jay Gatsby and Tom Buchanan will not get on - we just know it. Carraway's narration has prepared us for it, but also we know that Tom is a simmering centre of chaos waiting to explode and Gatsby is the rather unconventional hero, but hero nonetheless. In another scheme, Gatsby symbolises the carefree nouveau riche of the Jazz Age, whereas the Buchanans symbolise the smug, self-satisfied and immoral old money.

Such an understanding of character will allow your essays to be both sophisticated and multilayered; as well as helping you tick the required assessment objectives. Taking this more bird's eye approach will allow characters to be connected to prevailing themes. So continuing the examination of *The Great Gatsby* and *Frankenstein*, the various relationships between characters and thematic concerns creates a complex web of connections. For example, Frankenstein clearly embodies the theme of the egotistical overreacher, the man who should know his own limits. On another level he represents how knowledge can be dangerous in the wrong hands; how personal glory must always play second fiddle to the common good. The creature can be seen as a tool to explore social corruption of innocence, a pretty damning indictment of a 'civilised' Europe. Elizabeth represents the goodness and purity of the female as well as the wholesome necessity of health family relationships (suggested incest aside!). She can also be seen to allow considerations of how marginalised females are in patriarchal society, thus creating a surprising link with the creature that kills her.

Language and style

As you know, you must always ground your analysis in the hard evidence of textual fact. Illustrating your awareness of how a text creates an overall effect operating on different levels will certainly enhance your analysis and your essay marks. If you can establish **connections between the author's style and the themes they explore or the**

Nancy was on her way to school. As she walked along, she saw a little squirrel.

contextual concerns you will produce sophisticated literary analysis. So, we now dive back into the text to explain why considerations of language and style are crucial to examine.

What is style? How would you describe the way we have written this book and why do you think we have chosen this style? Despite what many might say it's not just because we do not know any other way! The questions you would ask to determine how we write are exactly the same questions you would seek to answer when trying to describe the style of any author. So some questions:

- Is the tone formal or informal? A concise way of thinking about this is informal writing would be the style you would use to email your friend about what happened at the weekend, whereas a formal style would be the way you would write an email to your local MP looking for them to ban essay writing from schools. Ours in a combination of both as we seek to keep a potentially dry subject matter engaging. We have to remember that we are writing an instructional text, which essentially is an extended exercise in us telling you what to do. Without a light, informal tone it might sound preachy and start to grate after the first few pages.

The giveaway with our style is the use of first person plural (we) and our use of direct address (you). We need to establish that we actually know what we're talking about and we constantly need to engage you the reader so we direct statements to you. Occasionally, you will see the use of "us", suggesting a connection between you, the reader, and us, as authors. This reinforces the unspoken common bond between us: we know what it's like having to write essays too. You pain is still our pain too! Additionally, is the tone serious or humorous or both? While we both have rather stunted senses of humour, we would like to think that there are instances where our writing is mildly amusing or interesting in some way.

- What type of language is used? Basically this refers to the complexity of expression really. If you are clicking "online dictionary" every few words, the author is using a complex vocabulary and this normally entails plenty of polysyllabic, Latinate words like "obscurantism" or "mellifluousness." In contrast, if you find that you are generally able to make your way through the text without any online help then the author is using a simple, accessible vocabulary that sounds very close to everyday speech, known as colloquial language. For reasons of clarity, we need to use simple language more often than not to make sure our meaning is clear.

- What type of sentences are used? Are they simple and to the point or are they long and complex. Hopefully, ours should be generally simple and concise. Why? Because we want to break down what can sometimes seem an impossible task into an array of smaller subtasks that can be understood easily and quickly. If you read a section and cannot understand the basic message, we have failed as writers.

Given the different ability range of readers we want every reader to understand, not just the most intelligent ones. Therefore simplicity is best. We also ask you lots of questions, don't we? Again, the aim is to engage not enrage. We ask questions not to make your life harder but to allow you access points to the material. This is the same reason we use lots of examples. Like mathematical equations, once you see these things in practical action they become much easier to understand and appreciate. However, some authors will use long flowing sentences and you must be prepared to pinpoint what effect they have.

Prose Under the Microscope

It might be a good idea to illustrate some different styles using actual authors. Two very contrasting styles can be found in the writers Ernest Hemingway and Angela Carter. See the section on recreative writing for more details on Carter. So let's have a look at an extract by each author:

> *It was late and every one had left the cafe except an old man who sat in the shadow the leaves of the tree made against the electric light. In the day time the street was dusty, but at night the dew settled the dust and the old man liked to sit late because he was deaf and now at night it was quiet and he felt the difference.*
>
> from *A Clean Well-Lighted Place;* Ernest Hemingway

> *I remember how, that night, I lay awake in the wagon - lit in a tender, delicious ecstasy of excitement, my burning cheek pressed against the impeccable linen of the pillow and the pounding of my heart mimicking that of the great pistons ceaselessly thrusting the train that bore me through the night, away from Paris, away from girlhood, away from the white, enclosed quietude of my mother's apartment, into the unguessable country of marriage.*
>
> from *The Bloody Chamber;* Angela Carter

Both of these are opening sentences and you can immediately sense the differences in style. How would you describe the differences between the two? It might be useful to answer the previous questions. Both authors have characteristic styles...

Hemingway writes in a deceptively simple, spare prose. His writing uses a basic vocabulary often with a domination of monosyllabic words. His sentences are usually short and very simple or are a series of such sentences joined by simple connectives like "and". In this case, the extract is full of details in the form of nouns with very few adjectives or adverbs are used to add qualifying detail. This is typical of Hemingway's style - a style he created to produce a new form of masculine writing shorn of fussy, busy description. **Hemingway's modernist style was a rejection of the more elaborate, information packed style of earlier Victorian novels** but also a response to his own experience as a soldier in World war One. What is also striking is the almost neutral, detached tone of the writing. It is a style called **minimalist** and rejects the idea of the author needing to provide huge layers of detail for the reader. In fact the reader must work quite hard to create the imaginative world of Hemingway's prose. In one sense, it may be likened to documentary filming. However, Hemingway's style means that readers must gather the little fragments of detail to construct an overall picture. It is almost poetic in its concise, densely packed description. Yet this works counter to the space that his simple style creates.

In this extract setting and characterisation is achieved very economically. He is "old" and "deaf" and symbolically sitting in "shadow." Later it is revealed that the man has attempted suicide. The darkness of the "shadow" also jars against the "clean, well-lighted" aspect of the title and as the story develops it becomes clear that such opposition of light and dark has a profound symbolic power associated with existential angst. But what of the "dust" and the

"quiet"? **In such a spare style every detail is significant**. Hemingway seems to be suggesting something about the commotion of the everyday, where serious thought is not possible. The "dust" also has a depressing connotation of the insignificance of humans and human life itself. However, what is interesting is how Hemingway's style and his use of polysyndeton (using lots of connectives) naturally brings the concepts of "dust" and "quiet" together. Instantly, on some level we are reminded of the Christian "ashes to ashes, dust to dust" refrain and suddenly the "quiet" the old man prefers takes on a much more significant status - the quiet of the big sleep itself.

Comparing this to Carter's extract, there is a very different feel to the writing. Gone is the detached simplicity. Instead, the presence of the "I" early on signals that this will be a much more emotional reading experience. Additionally, her sentence structure is much more complex. This is one single sentence crammed with details. In marked contrast to Hemingway, this is an

adjective overload. It's not just "excitement" she feels, it is a "tender, delicious ecstasy of excitement." **Carter writes in much more elaborate way which appears to be overwhelming compared to Hemingway**. It also reflects the overwhelming maelstrom of emotions that a naive young bride feels as she prepares herself for her deferred wedding night. Where Hemingway suggests detail through space, silence and displacement, Carter does this through providing lavish description, which the reader must examine meticulously. It is only with the same careful consideration needed to read Hemingway that the reader can discern what is important in Carter's writing.

The characterisation here is rich and abundant. The narrator is female and young ("girlhood") and unworldly and ("enclosed quietude") on the threshold of huge personal change (the repetition of "away"). As the story will go on to illustrate **Carter takes the typical Gothic heroine and twists her into something new**; updating the heroine to suit a feminist agenda. Instead of virtue in distress, we are presented with virtue in the distress

of desire. Carter uses vibrant symbolism in her fiction (as epitomised by the ruby choker the narrator wears later in the story that looks like a slit throat!). Here, there is a definite emphasis on sensuous description and this sensuality of style connects to the narrator's awakening sexuality. Look at the contrast of her "burning cheek" with the "impeccable linen" – a contrast of sexual passion and innocent experience which is further echoed through the colour symbolism of her "white, enclosed quietude." So, **stylistically it is clear that the sensuality of her ornate description, even in its soundscapes, and her vivid symbolism, which is dominated by the sense of smell and sight, combine to reflect the sensual overload experienced by the narrator**.

Furthermore, Carter cleverly employs symbolism to the theme of patriarchal violence that she explores through the story. Look at the phallic power of "the great pistons ceaselessly thrusting" her away into the "unguessable country of marriage." Even the train itself is phallic and the ceaseless thrusting foreshadows the violent taking of her virginity later in the story. However, **Carter skilfully utilises a long, winding sentence to suggest that the narrator's own stirring desires are somehow responsible for this sexual violence**; her "pounding" heart "mimicking" the train's pistons. In fact, the story could be viewed as a transformative rites of passage that realistically describes male sexual aggression but also reveals a more complex gender relationship than that of experienced, desiring males and innocent, desireless females. The female, too, is shown to desire sensual pleasure. But the horror of the attack suggests a need for rethinking such traditional sexual relations. All of which allows you to neatly connect Carter's style with her overall thematic exploration.

Narrative Structure

It is now time to look again at texts from the outside; to examine them from a more structural perspective. To those of you who may be a little shaky on this topic, you need to know the difference between the story and the plot. We would

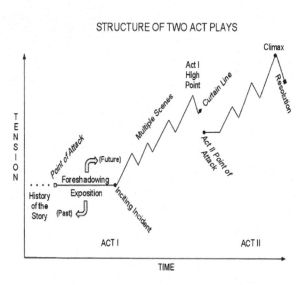

STRUCTURE OF TWO ACT PLAYS

recommend a quick read of the chapter on narratology in Peter Barry's *Beginning Theory* for a more in-depth examination. Essentially, the story is what you would tell a friend if they asked you to tell them what happens in Roddy Doyle's *The Woman Who Walked into Doors*. However, **the plot is really how that story (the chronological sequence of events) is actually sequenced and packaged by the author. The more technical name for plot is narrative structure** and, as you will know from films, how you tell the story is as important as the story itself. Have a look at Tarantino's *Pulp*

Fiction or Christopher Nolan's *Memento* for inspiration.

To take Doyle's novel as an example, why do you need to consider anything about its narrative structure? Because it is unique and should stand out as you read it. It is not a simple chronological narrative (not that there is anything wrong with chronological narratives at all). *The Woman Who Walked into Doors* alternates between the present and the past as the first person narrator, Paula Spencer,

attempts to tell her story. It is a very modern take on the traditional **bildungsroman** such as Charles Dickens' *David Copperfield* or Harper Lee's *To Kill a Mockingbird* or Joyce's *A Portrait of the Artist as a Young Man*. However, Doyle splices the narrative of Paula's present with an account of her past, always jumping from one to the other in a disorientating way. To further complicate things, there is another type of past narrative present: the short, sharp italicised chapters that disrupt this oscillating structure. Such chapters are fragments of description that capture the horrific domestic violence Paula has suffered.

But why is this important? On one level **Doyle's narrative structure highlights the interdependent relationship of past and present** and how the past clearly informs the present and will try to mould the future unless Paula takes control of her own destiny. On another level, **the brutal italic fragments puncture the narrative without warning and thus illustrate structurally the haunting nature of trauma**. No matter how hard Paula tries to cure her traumatised mind, the memories of the abuse she suffered strike without warning and with devastating effect. In this way, Doyle highlights how domestic abuse, in particular, and, trauma, in general, continue to plague the

124

victim; the initial traumatic event is only the starting point of suffering. Doyle's scathing indictment of Irish middle class complacency in the face of such social issues would have lacked the same memorability if told through a conventional chronological narrative structure by an omniscient narrator.

Again, **a useful way of trying to determine the importance of your chosen text's narrative structure is to imagine changing it substantially. You can then see what would be lost and gained in terms of how the reader interprets the story.** So if we removed Walton's letters from *Frankenstein*'s narrative, thereby destroying its closed framed structure; or rather than having three competing first person narrators we had just one, an omniscient narrator, how would things be different? If we removed the creature's narrative from its narrative womb at the centre of the story and ran it parallel to Victor's narrative, alternating between the two, what would happen? Maybe we could rearrange the narrative so it is strictly chronological. In this situation, Walton would not be encountered until the end and his elevation of Victor before he begins his story could not sway us in the same way.

Simply put, you as a student need to form a theory as to why the narrative structure chosen by the author best suits their thematic concerns. Do this and prove it with sensible argument and you are on the way to highly sophisticated analysis. Now we must claw our way out of the text and start to look at the intertextual factors you need to consider.

Intertextual Factors

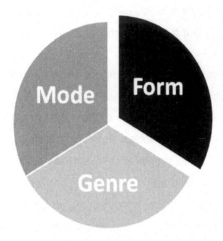

When it comes to consideration of intertextual factors the text you are analysing immediately becomes classified according to a number of helpful categories. Such categories are (most of the time) useful labels that help establish links with other texts quickly. The most common literary terms you need to be aware of are: **form**, **genre** and **mode**. The overlap and interchangeability of the terms form, genre and mode is discussed insightfully in chapter six of *Teaching English Literature 16-19: An Essential Guide* if you would like a terrifying journey into the black arts of classification (and teaching!). However, rather than enter into a debate about which one is most relevant when, it is easier to define them and show you how they can be used effectively.

To use a simple analogy, considering the intertextual factors is similar to an alien walking into a music store and considering the items on offer. The music [in our case, literature] comes in different **forms**. Music can be purchased on vinyl record or on CDs or accessed online through download codes. Either way these different forms relate to how literature also comes in different packages i.e. prose, poetry, drama.

Our curious alien may also be struck with how music is subdivided into **genres**. So whereas it may wander around the hip-hop or metal sections, we may organise literature into gothic prose fiction or pastoral poetry or comic drama and so on. Each category adheres to a certain established formula and such formulae are easily recognised. Hence it is easy enough to describe the characteristics of science fiction or Romantic poetry or Greek tragedy.

Another way that our alien friend might classify music might be through its intended effect on the listener. Thus the heartbreak of some soul ballads might be similar to the heart wrenching arias of some opera; the frenetic energy of psychobilly might seem very similar to the euphoria of rave. In literary terms such common tonal effects are described as literary **modes**. For example, the nihilistic bleakness of Mary Shelley's *Frankenstein* echoes with Alexander Pope's surreal and apocalyptic mock epic, *The Dunciad* in much the same way that William Blake's *London* connects to Cormac McCarthy's *The Road* or Henry Fielding's *Tom Jones* links to Jack Kerouac's *On The Road*. You get the general picture...

For your literary essays it is the form and genre that will play the more significant roles; although a consideration of modes between texts will provide quite useful connections. We do not intend to provide an encyclopaedia of various literary genres as it would be both very space consuming and also quite digressive. Once you have established the genre of your text(s) go away and find out about that genre and its characteristics, its exemplary texts and then consider how your chosen text engages with these genre expectations. We must apologise for risking a *Frankenstein* overkill here but it is a superb example of a text that utilises several sets of genre conventions. What genre best fits the novel - Gothic, Romantic, Science Fiction, Crime/Detective, travel writing, bildungsroman? Knowing the various characteristics of these genres and identifying how Shelley uses them allows the novel to be seen as a unique mutant text - a textual patchwork every bit as fascinating as the bodily mishmash of its legendary creation.

The remainder of this consideration of intertextual factors will examine the concept of literary forms.

Form

It might seem obvious, but you must draw attention to the form of your individual texts, especially if you are comparing prose with another form i.e. poetry or drama. When analysing literature at A-Level and beyond the basic forms are prose, poetry and drama. Some useful pointers on how to insightfully write about drama follow in chapter 15. In terms of our current focus on prose writing the two forms you will need to consider are the novel and the short story. However, form can also mean a type of layout (as in poetry). So the form of a novel could be described as epistolary, composed of letters, like Samuel Richardson's 1740 novel, *Pamela*. Each form operates differently and expects the reader to access meaning through different reading strategies; it is crucial that you display some awareness of these vital differences in your essays. For prose fiction you will have to consider the intratextual factors previously discussed [narrators, narrative perspective, language etc] but you will need to be aware that by necessity these devices operate differently in the novel than they do in the short story.

In order to write convincingly about short stories you must be able to understand them completely and on their own terms. **It is crucial that you understand how the short story operates before you consider its employment of narrative devices**. So, how does the short story differ from the prose novel apart from the glaringly obvious fact of being shorter? Obviously, it must operate in a much

shorter time frame than the novel and it cannot be as leisurely in achieving its effects. Narrative devices tend to be fewer in number, but are used more powerfully than in novels. Colin Barrett argues that *"the short story is closer to poetry than to the novel and despite their brevity, the best short stories require the same attentiveness from the reader – they cannot be browsed or skim-read."* A productive way of looking at short stories is to view them as the

climax of a novel but shorn of the preparatory and concluding detail that novels so usefully provide. Their ability to capture explosive and potentially transformative moments in ordinary lives was memorably captured by Anne Enright's description of fellow Irish writer John McGahern's stories as *"the literary equivalent of a hand grenade rolled across the kitchen floor."* Ultimately, Edna O'Brien states that a *"good short story has to hit like a bullet"* - an apt description of their **condensed and concise intensity**.

Due to their brevity, **short stories tend to plunge the reader into a situation, *in media res*, without preparation** *(in media res* is Latin for 'in the midst of things')*. Short stories also tend to reject the tying up of loose ends that novels can provide in a pleasing narrative closure. V.S. Pritchett, himself an expert short story writer, describes them as *"something glimpsed from the corner of the eye, in passing"*, which comes close to capturing the uncertainty, and the potential frustrations, that the unprepared reader can experience with short stories. As with all glimpses, they need to be re-examined to ascertain the truth of things. This fleeting quality of the short story is reflected in David Miller's excellent short story compendium, *That Glimpse of Truth*. Hence, **good short stories provide more questions than answers**. The best short stories haunt the reader after reading, lingering in the mind.

However, it is not only the unfamiliar brevity that can cause problems. **The type of characters that populate the short storm form are resolutely unheroic**. The protagonists found skulking in short stories are usually ordinary Joes/Josephines struggling to survive in the ordinary world. One is reminded of Leopold Bloom in James Joyce's sprawling novel *Ulysses*, whose heroism comes from his downright ordinariness. One could also look to the myriad, mundane characters populating Joyce's short story collection *Dubliners* i.e. Little Chandler, Gabriel Conroy, or Lenehan and Corley. While Frank O'Connor's assertion that "*the short story has never had a hero*" may be a little extreme, it is certainly fair to say that the majority of characters in short stories conform to Lynda Prescott's view of them as "*outsider figures who may have a sideways-on relationship with the society they inhabit*". Unpicking characterisation in short stories is a tricky process; **the rich nuanced layers of characterisation found in novels are simply not possible**.

Often the reader is left to work with comparatively few details and with incomplete pictures. Pritchett's language implied this; 'something' is vague, non-specific; this 'something' is only seen momentarily, 'glimpsed' and 'in passing'; and even then the something is not seen front on, in full view; rather

it is in the 'corner of the eye'. Hemingway, a master of the short story, whom we met previously, believed that:

"*If you leave out important things or events that you know about, the story is strengthened. [...] The test of any story is how very good the stuff that you, not your editors, omit.*"

Hemingway called this the iceberg theory where textual meaning is submerged deep below the surface of the text. Consequently, this necessitates high reader participation to fill in the gaps and silences of short stories and to quest for textual meaning. With this approach characteristic of the best short stories, it is no surprise that multiple meanings will be generated from such intense reader engagement. **This expectation can be seen as a laborious chore by some or as a fulfilling detective game by others.**

But what is the reward of this extra reader interaction? A.L. Kennedy describes how the "*short story has a way of catching the precise moment when a heart is defined, a soul is broken, a*

joy named. These are fictions that bring you right home to the size, threat and wonder of reality" whereas Frank O'Connor sees them as fictions where "*people are presented in rather intense, isolated moments which retrospectively radiate a profound sense of human significance*". **Due to their intense conciseness short stories must be combed through with a forensic eye, reinforcing the role of the reader as a literary detective solving the puzzle with the fragments of clues provided by the author.** Such high reader participation is also required when writing about drama, as will be explained in the next section.

Once you have grasped the fundamental differences between the short story and its longer prose siblings then it is a matter of repeating the inspection of narrative devices discussed previously.

Extratextual Factors

See Part the Third, chapters 18 and 19: How to use critics and critical theory.

Contextual Factors

See Part the Third, chapter 20: How to use context.

15. Writing about Drama

Drama can be a tricky engagement for the skilled literature student mainly because of its particular type of form. Plays might seem quick, relatively easy reads but some students genuinely struggle to write successfully about dramatic texts. Part of the problem is due to a play's relative sparseness of detail. **Drama texts are no more than scripts with dialogue and the occasional stage direction and scene description. Drama**  **texts cannot provide the wealth of environmental description or characterisation that prose texts can**. Yet they must fundamentally tell similar narratives with similarly meaningful themes.

To draw another analogy from sci-fi classic *The Matrix* the drama text is similar to the training construct that Keanu Reeves finds himself in - a white room that must be imaginatively furnished. When reading drama, the reader is required to put in substantial imaginative effort to turn the two-dimensional nature of a script into a three-dimensional stage version. **Drama texts rarely tell the reader where characters move, what they are wearing, what their facial expressions are, what their body language is like or what the set looks like**.

Often in plays some characters will not be speaking, but still be present on stage. How these witnesses react to what's going on affects, and may even shape, the audience's response. Yet typically there will be no reference to their actions/reactions in the script. For example, at the start of scene two of *Hamlet,* the king, Claudius, is leading the celebrations of his coronation and dealing publicly with an outbreak of international conflict. The positive mood Claudius hopes to generate is seriously undermined by the silent presence of his nephew, a brooding figure, dressed in funeral black. A theatre director could draw our attention to Hamlet's contempt for his uncle's performance in a number of ways; by placing Hamlet downstage, nearer to the audience; by having other characters watch Hamlet closely, by his different costume and so on. The point is that none of these things are indicated by stage directions in the script, though Claudius' anxiety about his nephew is implied in his speech. Such gaps in drama texts mean that they are even more open to different interpretations than novels or poems. **If you don't think about the visual dimensions of drama you may as well be reading a radio play.** For a more sustained discussion of stagecraft see the discussion of Tennessee Williams' *A Streetcar Named Desire* later in this section.

Obviously, it is not easy to conjure up such dramatic worlds unprepared. Hence we fully believe that **the more drama you see in production the more you will appreciate all the decisions that must be made to transform an inanimate script into a living stage production.** Whether this involves frequent forays to the theatre or comparing different film versions of the same play it all amounts to the same thing - an increased awareness of the different strategies of bringing a play to its audience. **Having a basic appreciation of the theatrical space and what can be done with it is key. If you know the possibilities available for lighting and sound and costume or the different theatrical devices used for tragedy, as opposed to comedy, your readings of drama will become much more fruitful.** It is important to recognise the playscript for what it is - a skeleton which must be embellished but which gives the essential shape of the drama.

So what do you need to be aware of when writing about a play? At the most basic levels you are concerned with the type of concerns familiar from prose - setting, characterisation, pace and tension and so forth.

Characterisation

More than any other literary form drama will speak through character the most, so an awareness of characterisation is essential. What characters say and how they say it, what other characters say about each other, how they behave and what their role is in the play overall, how they connect to the major themes of the play will all be essential knowledge. This should all be evident from the script itself. However, your own imagining of the play will help to reinforce the clues you pick up from the play itself.

For example, take Eugene O'Neill's odd modernist expressionist play *The Hairy Ape*, written in 1922. The protagonist is an unlikeable ship worker called Yank, a bully of a man who commands respect through intimidation. He is uneducated, working class and ignorant - a strange choice for a tragic hero. O'Neill reveals his character through:

THE HAIRY APE

1. <u>detailed stage directions</u>: "*Yank is seated foreground. He seems broader, fiercer, more truculent, more powerful, more sure of himself than the rest. They respect his superior strength - the grudging respect of fear.*" Stage directions will be visually distinct from the dialogue on the page; as above they are usually, though not always, in italics. Stage directions always contain key information, so be attentive to them.

2. <u>what Yank says:</u> "What d'yuh want wit home? [*Proudly*] I runned away from home when I was a kid. On'y too glad to beat it, dat was me. Home was lickings for me, dat's all. But yuh can bet your shoit no one ain't ever licked me since! Wanter try it, any of youse? Huh!"

3. <u>how he says it</u>, which will be suggested by a combination of stage directions and the reader's understanding of the character's situation: "[*Standing up and glaring at Long*] Sit down before I knock you down!"

4. <u>how he treats others</u>, in this case the old Irish sailor, Paddy: "Aw, yuh crazy Mick! [*He springs to his feet and advances on PADDY threateningly - then stops, fighting some queer struggle within himself - lets his hands fall to his sides contemptuously*] Aw take it easy. Yuh're aw right at dat. Yuh're bugs, dat's all - nutty as a cuckoo."

5. <u>the reaction of others to him</u>, this is from Yank's confrontation with the New York upper classes:

   YANK: [...] [*He swaggers away and deliberately lurches into a top-hatted gentleman, then glares at him pugnaciously*] Say, who d'yuh tink yuh're bumpin'? Tink yuh own de oith?
   GENTLEMAN: [*coldly and affectedly*] I beg your pardon. [*He has not looked at YANK and passes on without a glance, leaving him bewildered*]

Yank is an aggressive, ill-educated man used to settling his problems through violence and intimidation. As becomes very clear from the play, rational thinking and patience are not his specialities. He is a big fish in a very small pond and when he comes to New York seeking retribution he becomes a minnow in an ocean of powerful social sharks. Inevitably, he cannot comprehend or cope with his new-found powerlessness and the play explores his attempts to change this and regain his previous supremacy. Clearly, O'Neill has sketched out the essentials for us, but the specifics of what he looks like on stage, how and where he moves is up to you. When you're reading a play, try to think of yourself as directing it in the theatre of your imagination.

There are specialised types of character speech that you need to be aware of too. A character indulging in an extended speech to himself alone on stage is called a **soliloquy**. While in the real world this might prove of grave medical concern, on the stage it is an opportunity for the playwright to externalise the interior world of the character. The most obvious examples are from Shakespeare's many tragic heroes, the most famous being procrastinating Hamlet's "to be or not to be" speech. In complete contrast to this is the rapid-fire rapport between characters that can signify comic wit or high conflict. This rapid alteration of speaker, usually with single line, originates in Greek tragedy and has a suitably Greek name - **stichomythia**. Like the novelist, the playwright will vary pace and suspense on various levels. The situations and clash of characters they create is the most obvious way. However, the content as well as the layout of the dialogue can do this too. **By their very nature, soliloquies slow down pace, whereas stichomythia quickens it. However the content of the dialogue will determine the suspense**.

Oscar Wilde's quick-fire comic rapport in *The Importance of Being Earnest* creates farce rather than tension, whereas Aeschylus's use of rapid dialogue in *Seven Against Thebes* ratchets up the tension until it emerges that the brothers Polynices and Eteocles must face each other at the seventh gate. Shakespearian soliloquies, while slowing down the pace, are used to increase tension by allowing the audience access to character motivations, which clearly point the way to impending tragedy.

Stage directions allow playwrights to supply essential information that cannot be transmitted through character dialogue. A classic example is JB Priestley's instruction in *An Inspector Calls* for the lighting to change from

a soft pink hue to a harsh white to signify the arrival of the eponymous inspector and the interrogation he brings for the complacent Birling family. Usually written in italics to differentiate from character dialogue stage directions can be invaluable sources of

information. An interesting stage direction associated with character dialogue is **the aside**, which allows a character to directly address the audience without the knowledge of the other characters. The **breaching of the so-called fourth wall (that separates the fictional world of the stage from the real world of the audience) creates complicity between character and audience allowing the playwright to exploit all types of dramatic irony** for comic effect or to reveal ulterior character motivations not previously known.

Scene locations are clearly limited to some extent in drama compared to the boundless possibilities of prose, due to the practicalities of the stage itself. However, **it is most important to observe the different scene changes as they are often used as a patterning device by playwrights.** In *The Hairy Ape* O'Neill uses the scene locations to create patterns of opposites. The opening scene in the worker's mess is sharply contrasted to the airy upper deck of the affluent passengers of Mildred and her aunt. The furnace that Yank feeds furiously reflects the dangerous atmosphere building around him. Removing Yank from where he naturally "belongs" i.e. from the bowels of the ship to the jewellery shops on Fifth Avenue highlights his existential alienation. Finally, his experiences in the monkey house of the city zoo underline the irony of his tragic condition.

Again, to discuss the finer intricacies of acting would necessitate a completely separate book and we have no intention of pursuing this venture at present. However, we think a discussion of a concrete example will help to illustrate the vital importance of both imagining the types of stagecraft decisions possible when reading and also noting the stagecraft decisions made when you watch productions yourself.

Stagecraft Discussed: *A Streetcar Named Desire*

Tennessee Williams' 1947 tragedy of the destruction of Southern belle, Blanche Dubois, is one of the most performed plays of the 20th Century [and probably 21st too]. **Famous for its heroine slumming it in a steamy, claustrophobic New Orleans ghetto and her subsequent conflict with alpha male brother-in-law, Stanley Kowalski, it is a cocktail of heat, desire, deception and madness.** It is the play that made the actor Marlon Brando famous, whose legacy is an almost impossible role to surpass for all budding wanna-be Stanleys.

Most productions follow the excellent 2013 production directed by Ethan McSweeny, with its faithful reproduction of a typical 1947 rundown neighbourhood and characteristic cramped two bedroom apartment. This version, starring Lia Williams as Blanche, retained the period costumes and the realism for which most productions strive. Its most impressive aspect, apart from Williams' stunning performance as Blanche, was to use the original play's prioritising of music as a way of joining separate scenes. **Between scenes a vocalist, accompanied by a clarinettist, performed live songs that musically bridged scenes – both extending their mood and anticipating new ones.**

This stagecraft decision in not indicated in Williams' [Tennessee this time] stage directions despite the use of music being a significant indicator of emotional tone in the play. In the play we encounter stage directions of this nature:

- *"The music of the 'blue piano' grows louder."*
- *"The rapid, feverish polka tune, the 'Varsouviana,' is heard."*
- *"The sound of it turns into an approaching locomotive."*
- *"The hot trumpet and drums from the Four Deuces sound loudly."*

As Blanche's mental state unravels the music becomes more and more intrusive, disrupting the realism of the action with the surrealism of her madness. In McSweeny's production, **the live jazz and blues performances further emphasised and articulated both the sultry, sensuality of the New Orleans location and the tragic sadness of Blanche's breakdown.** This musical colour was also matched by vibrant colourful lighting where deep sensuous purples and rich passionate  reds created the type of world corresponding to Blanche's projected self-delusions.

However, a radically different approach to the play's setting was taken by director Benedict Andrews in 2014. Breaking with tradition, he created an ultra-modern New Orleans setting. **His approach to the stagecraft of the play was to ditch the realism and emphasise the artifice of the spectacle.** To this end by staging the play in the round (i.e. the audience surrounds the

spectacle of the drama itself) his production destroyed the so-called 'fourth wall' that the audience usually occupies. Additionally, his entire stage set rotated at slow speed so that the audience was confronted with a constantly moving performance that never allowed the audience to get fully comfortable. To accommodate this, the two-room apartment became a space with no walls but with furniture and doors. Seen from far away it resembled a type of sterile cage. While allowing maximum visibility for the almost intrusive audience, it also emphasised the complete lack of privacy that Blanche suffers in her new cramped abode.

Overall, the audience became much more engaged as it strained to see the expressions of the actors, to hear their lines and to put all these pieces together. **The overall effect was to increase the voyeuristic nature of the audience and cleverly draw them closer to the action.** This blending together or unrealistic setting with realistic action also emphasised the unstable boundaries between reality and fantasy, safety and threat that characterise the play. The transgression of these supposedly separate boundaries as indicated by William's use of music and flashback [the fatal gunshots that echo through the play and Blanche's fraying mind] thus found reinforcement through the staging of this production.

Much is made of lighting in the play as Blanche's paranoia about her fading looks ensures hysteria about lighting inside the transparent apartment; most memorably when Mitch "tears the paper lantern off the light bulb." In Andrews' production, the lighting was vibrant and varied with the entire stage bathed in different coloured pastel hues for the main dramatic action and much more intense luminous blues and purples between scene changes. So, **a whole spectrum of colour from soft whites and yellows to explosive purples and greens was employed to create an intoxicating visual spectacle**. The constant colour changes combined and clashed, thus adding to the dynamic conflicts of the production and preventing the audience from settling into complacence.

The famous paper lantern prop that hides reality for Blanche was coloured red in this production, which became a colour motif throughout the play as Blanche swanned around in a bright red silk gown in certain scenes and towards the end donned a red dress with an almost childlike red bow in her hair. However, **the colour schema achieved through costume colour was more intricate than first meets the eye**. Blanche's red silk dressing gown was matched by Stella's bright red pyjama shorts and most strikingly by Stanley's bright red silk pyjamas before the infamous rape scene. A fascinating colour symmetry between Stella and Blanche was created by their clothing at the beginning and end of the play. When Blanche first comes to Elysian Fields Stella wore a bright yellow top with light blue leggings and when Blanche left the play mentally destroyed she wore a bright yellow dress with a light blue jacket. This colour connection subtly symbolised the inversion of the sisterly hierarchy in the play as Blanche shifted from initial dominance to final vulnerability. By the play's end it was the little sister who looked after the big sister, not the other way round. Such subtle visual connections were also echoed in the soundscapes that Andrews employed.

The jazz music that dominates the original script was rejected by Andrews as he incorporated more contemporary music. One notable scene that dramatised the intense sexual attraction smouldering between Stella and Stanley was not mentioned in the stage directions, but added much to the portrayal of the intense desires that swirl around the tiny apartment. This sequence was used to bridge between two scenes in a way that both distracted the audience from the dead time between scene changes as well as adding to the play's thematic explorations of sex and domination between men and women. Here Vanessa Kirby, as Stella, and Ben Foster, as Stanley, engaged in a carefully choreographed and stylised sex scene accompanied by the guitar riff from PJ Harvey's "To Bring You My Love." **The slow sensuous guitar motif set the pace for the deliberately slowed down movement of the actors and it brought a dark, striking physicalisation of what the play suggests rather than dramatises**. Tellingly, Stella was very much dominated by Stanley as Kirby was led by Foster to their bed; her subservience  underscored by her physical location below Foster. Even the title of Harvey's song, sung by a female, seemed quite apt, to the female role in this brief scene, where love is traded for sexual satisfaction. Elsewhere, ear-assaulting blasts of guitar feedback courtesy of Jimi Hendrix perforated the performance space between scene changes to mirror the disorientating colour changes.

The strategy of contemporary music was continued by using Chris Isaac's famous "Wicked Game" to reflect the loss of hope experienced by Blanche towards the end of the play.

Combined with such bold lighting and sound decisions the actors also played a significant role in stagecraft decisions. **They became a manifestation of stagecraft in action through their gestures, delivery, stage position etc**.

Gillian Anderson, for example, played Blanche in a highly effective way. For the first half of the play her Blanche grated on the nerves with her affectations of gentility, childishness and coquetry by presenting almost a Southern stereotype. She prioritised her self-delusion and feigned confidence; epitomised by her entrance in designer sunglasses, designer outfit and huge heels. Anderson's performance, however, was subtle; an underlying discomfort and anxiety oozed through the veneer of confidence; through laughter that was just slightly too manic, twitching hand gestures, restless body movements and an airiness of delivery that seemed to fade to a sigh at times. However, **as the second half commenced Blanche's artifice died away and Anderson played up the reality of her emotional turmoil**. The disjunction between the annoying and immature Blanche and the subsequently exposed and vulnerable Blanche maximised audience sympathy by her sudden and rapid collapsing fortunes.

For the rape scene the decision to have Blanche change into an ill-fitting ball gown and tiara complete with smeared make-up was both visually and emotionally highly effective. It showed Blanche desperately and misguidedly still trying to perpetuate her own prom-queen delusions while also revealing the inappropriateness of such delusions. The ghastly Joker-esque lipstick that

Anderson applied so disastrously further emphasised Blanche's unhinged mental state. **Anderson's frantic scuttling up and down the apartment, wheeling and circling with over exaggerated movements contrasted perfectly with Foster's cool, calculated movements as they dramatised the focused predator hunting a skittish prey**. Foster maximised Stanley's alpha male status at the start of the play when he delivered a bag of red meat to Stella covered in grease and dirt and his primal desires were embodied further when Foster navigated his way through the under-netting of Blanche's ball gown with calculating menace. Without showing the actual sexual violence itself it was a highly effective way of disturbing the audience and propelling Blanche towards her tragic end.

The contrast between Anderson's appearance as she entered and exited the play could not be more marked. **She entered with the air of a cool, confident, glamorous woman replete with heels, sunglasses, styled hair and designer gear and exited a broken woman with lank, unbrushed hair, smudged lipstick and faraway gaze**. Anderson also prolonged Blanche's tragic exit by slowly walking all the way around the revolving stage to maximise both the spectacle of her departure as well as audience sympathy.

Now that you have been initiated into the dark arts of stagecraft as well as refreshing your knowledge of intratextual devices, it might be wise to see them put into action. The new A-Level specifications require a close textual analysis of unseen passages, so it makes sense to apply this to drama texts, texts that require an additional awareness of stagecraft and of how different directors, actors and audeinces can interpret a text. As elsewhere, knowledge of various productions will also help you to answer this sort of question fully.

<u>*Othello*: Analysis of an Unseen Extract from a Shakepeare play</u>

This task features on a number of the new specifications at both AS and A-Level, including AQA A, AQA B and WJEC. Though the AQA tasks examine the selected passage through specific lenses (spec. A through the thematic lens of love; spec. B through the genre of tragedy), the main focus for the examination questions is on the presentation of characters through language. All the questions also test AO 1 and AO2 - the quality of understanding and close reading of language.

We're going to work through one example on *Othello* taken from AQA's specimen assessment material. Though the approach we take has AQA's style of question in mind it should be easily adaptable to other specifications.

Before we plunge in, a quick word of advice on the structure of your essay. As we've emphasised elsewhere in this book, in all close reading exercises, on poetry, drama or prose, **we strongly** advise that your essay does not work chronologically through the text from opening to final line. Nor should you try to summarise the action. If your essay starts with 'in the first line of the text' or you find yourself using chronological discourse markers, such as 'then', 'after', 'before' and 'when' you'll know you're losing your analytical focus and your examiner will be tutting and muttering darkly to themselves. A paragraph starting 'Then Othello says to Iago that...' is likely to develop into narrative summary. This is always to be avoided as it's worth very few marks.

In contrast, examiners will be delighted by, and handsomely reward, perceptive, assured close reading that is well informed by your studies. By perceptive they mean spotting what is not immediately obvious, reading between the lines, picking up subtext, being alert to the nuances of technique and specific choices of language. 'Assured' suggests your reading should be rooted in strong knowledge and understanding of the text and of ways of reading it.

AQA B Specimen Question: Othello – William Shakespeare
Explore the significance of the aspects of dramatic tragedy in the following passage in relation to the play as a whole. [25 marks]

You should consider the following in your answer:
- the presentation of Iago and Othello
- the dramatic setting
- other relevant aspects of dramatic tragedy.

Venice Outside the Saggitary
Enter Othello, Iago, attendants with torches

IAGO
Though in the trade of war I have slain men,
Yet do I hold it very stuff o'th' conscience
To do no contrived murder: I lack iniquity
Sometimes to do me service. Nine or ten times

I had thought t'have yerked him here under the ribs.

OTHELLO
'Tis better as it is.

IAGO
Nay, but he prated
And spoke such scurvy and provoking terms
Against your honour,
That with the little godliness I have,
I did full hard forbear him. But I pray, sir,
Are you fast married? For be assured of this,
That the Magnifico is much beloved,
And hath in his effect a voice potential
As double as the Duke's. He will divorce you,
Or put upon you what restraint and grievance
That law, with all his might to enforce it on,
Will give him cable.

OTHELLO
Let him do his spite:
My services, which I have done the signory,
Shall out-tongue his complaints. 'Tis yet to know –
Which, when I know that boasting is an honour,
I shall provulgate – I fetch my life and being
From men of royal siege, and my demerits
May speak, unbonneted, to as proud a fortune
As this that I have reached. For know, Iago,
But that I love the gentle Desdemona,
I would not my unhousèd free condition
Put into circumscription and confine
For the seas' worth. But look, what lights come yond!

IAGO
Those are the raisèd father and his friends:
You were best go in.

OTHELLO Not I: I must be found.
My parts, my title, and my perfect soul
Shall manifest me rightly. Is it they?

IAGO
By Janus, I think no.
Enter Cassio, with men bearing torches

OTHELLO
The servants of the Duke and my Lieutenant!
The goodness of the night upon you, friends.
What is the news?

CASSIO
The Duke does greet you, General,
And he requires your haste-post-haste appearance
Even on the instant.

OTHELLO
What is the matter, think you?

CASSIO
Something from Cyprus, as I may divine:
It is a business of some heat. The galleys
Have sent a dozen sequent messengers
This very night at one another's heels;
And many of the consuls, raised and met,
Are at the Duke's already. You have been hotly called for,
When being not at your lodging to be found.
The senate hath sent about three several quests
To search you out.

OTHELLO
'Tis well I am found by you:
I will but spend a word here in the house
And go with you.

Exit
(Act 1, Scene 2)

It's possible that over time AQA will advise candidates to answer each of the three bullet points in sequence, perhaps even separately. Who knows? But, for now, we're going to assume that the response required is a coherent essay which treats the bullet points as prompts for discussion. We should point out that what follows isn't in itself meant to be an exemplar answer. See it rather as a guide to the sort of analysis the boards are after.

Where should we start our response? As we've said before in our section on introductions, it's helpful to begin with an overview. **Establish the big picture first**. In your introduction outline the aspects which you're going to go on to examine more closely in the main body of the essay. In this instance, we'd start with contexts. The scene is from Act 1 Scene 2 so comes very early in the play; indeed it is the first time Othello appears on stage. Crucially, however, he has already been described by Iago and Roderigo in the previous scene, so **expectations about his character have already been established and could now be confirmed, or confounded**. The play's narrative structure is also significant: we also already know that Iago secretly hates Othello and is plotting against him. Hence this scene is full of dramatic irony; we, the audience, know Iago is duplicitous; Othello and the other characters do not.

Notice how Shakespeare has to strike a delicate dramatic balance in his use of dramatic irony: Iago must perform the role of dutiful, loyal servant convincingly enough for the other characters to believe in it. However, Shakespeare also needs to signal to the audience what Iago is really up to – **trying to sow seeds of contention between Othello and other characters and in the process undermine his master's authority, without this being obvious**. If this signalling is too overt Othello will be made to look a fool and the audience will lose sympathy for the tragic hero.

For AQA B, we've also to consider this scene through the lens of tragedy. So we should comment on the fact that **the scene features the tragic hero and hints at a number of potential causes of his downfall**. For instance, external forces, such as a villainous enemy, Othello's outsider status in Venice (he is a Moor in a Christian culture) and the wider context of conflict (between Venice and Turkey, as introduced by Cassio). Aristotle's term 'harmatia' refers  to a flaw in the protagonist or the protagonist's behaviour. Potential internal sources of tragedy could include Othello's difficulty in perceiving Iago's double dealing, arguably his arrogance or even hubris (psychological flaws) as well as the potentially poor decisions he makes, specifically secretly marrying Desdemona, promoting Cassio over Iago and then trusting Iago.

On to the setting. Here the setting is a street in the city state of Venice outside an inn, in darkness. Each of these three details is significant as we will go on to show. We're sure you'll be able to say something about the importance of Venice, particularly for a Renaissance audience. Limit your consideration of Venice to one or two sentences and make it relevant to this passage, as contextual information simply regurgitated from notes would set the examiner frowning again. Broadly, for Shakespeare's contemporaries Venice denotes a cultured, orderly and civilised society, potentially under threat from what they considered to be non-Christian barbarians. The fact that Othello is the 'Moor of Venice' resonates with this socio-political context. The fact that he is found outside an inn, in the streets is also significant. Inns

in Shakespeare's plays are often associated with low life characters and rough, sordid action. **This is not the natural or fitting location for noble characters or noble behaviour. Thus it creates some tension**. Darkness obviously adds to this, literally making characters and the audience uncertain about what is happening, but also symbolically suggesting immorality, dark deeds, ignorance and so forth.

How does the setting link to the characters? This setting certainly suits Iago's machiavellian character and dark machinations. What else do we learn about him in this scene? Firstly he's a great actor; he can perform different roles dextrously. Iago requires Othello to believe he is a straightforward, plain-speaking, reliable and loyal soldierly servant. So this is how he presents himself. Hence his speech about being provoked to violently defend Othello's honour and his soldierly ethical distinctions about killings in battle and in civilian life. **Underneath the mask of solid reliability and loyal concern, however, Iago quickly stokes unease, insinuating that Othello's marriage may be the cause of violent discord between the Moor and the most powerful figures in Venice**.

Iago's first attempts to unsettle Othello fail, so he has to up the rhetorical ante. Employing emotive and inflammatory language, he utilises imagery of disease: 'such scurvy and provoking terms'. Notice how unspecific Iago is about the details. He does not tell us what had actually been said or by whom or why he was almost driven to murder. **Presenting themselves as transparently informative, Iago's words are actually hooks, baited to snag Othello and tug at his self-assurance**. The pun on 'fast' to mean hasty, but also secure, for instance, attempts to shake Othello's confidence in his marriage, a tactic Iago will develop further as the play goes on. Iago also introduces legal language to imply that Othello might be arrested for his actions, 'restraint', 'law', 'grievance' and 'enforce'. His reaction to the appearance of the torches ('You had best go in') is typical of how he pretends

to be acting to protect Othello's best interests, but actually seeks to stir up and exacerbate all the trouble he can. Hence his claim that the torches are being carried by Branbantio and his followers.

Why does Iago swear 'by Janus', a double-headed God who simultaneously looks in opposite directions? Perhaps Shakespeare gives him this line to **ensure the theatre audience has properly**

understood Iago's double-dealing nature. Possibly an inattentive audience could have been taken in by Iago's impressive impersonation of honest servant. Plays are written to be performed, obviously, and different directors and actors will interpret characters differently. Iago could, for instance, be played as a rather nervous character, on edge in case his villainy is discovered. Or he could be played as a confident smiling machiavel, a villain who takes sadistic pleasure from hoodwinking his master with such consummate ease. In this second interpretation 'by Janus' could be performed as a sort of metaphorical nudge and wink to the audience, a 'look at me, see what I'm doing?' – Iago enjoying vaunting his true diabolical nature right under Othello's nose.

This leads us to consider how we react to Iago at this point in the play. Later, of course, we will be taken into his plans and made queasily complicit in them through Shakespeare's use of soliloquies. But even here, different readers and audiences will respond differently, in part depending on how the

characters are played. **We might, for instance, be impressed by Iago's skill and cleverness, or we may already be repulsed by his betrayal of his noble master**. Our reaction to Iago depends largely on how we respond to Othello.

As we have already mentioned, Othello has already been described in scene 1 through the poisonous, racist perspective of Iago and Roderigo. How he appears in this scene belies this impression. Othello's first words in the play, for instance, are simple and direct, contrasting in their calmness with Iago's urgent agitated tone. **The tragic hero's composure and control of the**

situation is evinced by the way he interrupts Iago's line, halting the hurried onward flow of words and rhythm with five emphatic monosyllables: 'Let him do his spite'. Later when the torches are seen and Iago tries to unnerve Othello by implying there might be violent trouble – 'you were best go in' – Othello is again unflustered, using similarly direct language to emphasise this command: 'Not I, I must be found'.

Generally Othello's style of speech is declarative, measured, at times, rather grand. **He comes across as a character that is used to being listened to. We learn that his self-assurance rests on his royal heritage and the brave deeds he has done**. There is, however, some indication of a chink in his armour; his admission that he is not totally familiar yet with Venetian cultural etiquette (he has not broadcast his heritage as yet because he is unsure about whether this boasting would be deemed dishonourable). Later in the  play Iago will, of course, turn Othello's outsider status against him. Another potential Achilles heel is his marriage to Desdemona, which Othello admits may in some ways 'confine' him and make him vulnerable to control, 'circumscription'. This acknowledgement of potential weakness is, of course, music to Iago's ears and ammunition for his scheming.

Othello's elevated idiom and elegant syntax may be distinct from Iago's plainer language in this scene, but they share a soldierly mentality. We see this in Othello's claim that his actions will speak for him ('my services…shall out-tongue') and in his **reference to 'unbonneted', a metaphor that suggests he values language that is plain, not dressed up or disguised in any way**. It is part of a group of phrases in this passage that highlight the

153

importance of language: 'He prated'; 'provoking terms'; 'a voice'; 'out-tongue'. As we shall see later in the play, Othello's noble actions will be fatally undermined by Iago's brilliant use of words as masks and weapons.

Perhaps then, there is a certain naivety to Othello that could be read as his hamartia. In particular, he is naïve in trusting Iago and about how he is viewed in Venice. He also trusts Iago's words because they are dressed plainly. Isn't there also something arrogant too about his self-assurance? His reference to his 'perfect soul' seems, in particular, hubristic.

Overall in this short extract **Othello is presented as a tower of strength, a tower that Venetian society depends on when threatened by external enemies**. The foundations of Othello's strength rest on his noble relationships with other characters. As the play develops he will lean ever more heavily on one of these characters, his faithful seeming servant 'honest' Iago. We know, of course, that Iago is in fact constantly chipping away at those foundations in order that, eventually, the tower will topple, and seemingly of its own accord.

Once you start to master such nuanced discussion of the intratextual factors you find in your drama text then you must ask yourself a very important extratextual question: "Is this a comedy or a tragedy?"

Dramatic Genre: Tragedy or Comedy...or Both?
This essentially describes the feel of the play you are reading and you must be able to tune into how these feelings are created for the audience. **Essentially, tragedies are dramas of loss and sadness whereas comedies are dramas of confusion and laughter**. Comedies are often sensibly described as anti-tragedies and vice versa.

Comedy and tragedy have coexisted from the earliest origins of Western literature. In Classical Greece, Homer's epic tragedy *The Iliad* existed alongside a comic parody known as *The Battle of Frogs and Mice*. **Even the** great Athenian tragedians Aeschylus, Sophocles and Euripides complimented their great tragic trilogies with a riotous and raucous satyr play. This equalising of the two genres can also be seen in Shakespeare's output where the comedy occupies a significant proportion of his work. In fact, Shakespeare notably introduces comic elements to some of his tragedies [see the sexual innuendo laden lads' banter of *Romeo and Juliet*!] or the darkness that makes his comedy *Measure for Measure* so unusual.

However, as always, **the view of tragedy and comedy as mutually exclusive genres can be challenged by playwrights who seek to blend these seemingly binary opposites together**. Erma Bombeck highlights not their separateness but rather their closeness when she states that "there is a thin line that separates laughter and pain, comedy and tragedy, humour and hurt." This has becomes especially prominent after World War Two where Samuel Beckett can describe his *Waiting for Godot* as a "tragicomedy in two acts." Anyone who has seen this darkly comic play "where nothings happens twice" will recognise Beckett's successful blending of black comedy and existential tragedy. In fact, the play teaches its audience that laughter is the antidote to the tragic existential angst that haunts its characters.

Without enrolling you on a very long university degree in dramatic genre we will do the next best thing in the space allotted: a whistle stop guided tour of these seemingly alien lands of comedy and tragedy. It is essential that you know how to recognise their unique features when reading and writing about them.

Tragedy

This is an enormous subject and we're going to try to squeeze it into just a few pages. Necessarily, therefore, our approach is introductory not comprehensive, an invitation to further reading. We'll begin by trying to define tragedy and then go on to outline key ideas and concerns connected with the genre.

What is a tragedy?

'Double denim is a fashion tragedy' prompts the question as to whether it is possible, necessary or desirable, to distinguish between the common and literary meaning of the word 'tragedy'. Look it up in a good reference book and you'll find something along the lines of the following distinction:

- A serious incident, crime or natural catastrophe
- A literary text dramatising tragic events, with an unhappy ending, including the death or downfall of the protagonist.

So it appears there may be a clear distinction between the common and literary usage. Literary reference books often offer further confirmation: according to *The Complete A-Z English Literature Handbook*, for example, a tragedy is a 'drama which ends disastrously' and falls into two broad types:

- Greek tragedy, where fate brings about the downfall of the character(s)

- Shakespearean tragedy, where a character has free will and their fatal flaw causes the downfall'.

Seeking to make the distinction sharper, the American playwright, **Arthur Miller, argued that there's a clear difference between what he called the 'pathetic' (the common use of the word 'tragic') and the literary meaning of 'tragic'** and that these different meanings are evinced by the different emotions reactions of the reader/audience. Miller gives the following helpful example:

> '*When Mr. B, while walking down the street, is struck on the head by a falling piano, the newspapers call this is a tragedy. In fact, of course, this is only the pathetic end of Mr. B. Not only because of the accidental nature of his death; that is elementary. It is pathetic because it merely arouses our feelings of sympathy, sadness and possibly identification. What the death of Mr. B. does not arouse is tragic feeling.*'

Put on your dramatist's thinking cap for a moment and consider how you might develop this pathetic scenario into something truly, profoundly tragic. (You're going to have to get cruel to do this, so steel yourself gentle reader.) Would it make any difference, for example, if you had other characters also killed by the giant piano? Perhaps an old lady who'd stopped to catch her breath. Or what if you did not kill Mr. B off instantly, but added instead a scene of him battling bravely, but of course hopelessly, against fatal injuries? What if you added a grieving wife and children into the scene? Surely that would wring sadness out of even the hardest-hearted of audiences. But the tone will also be vital; sympathy for the protagonist is essential in tragedies, but not in comedies. **Tragedy and comedy may appear to be binary opposites, but notice how easily our scenario could slip into parody or farce**. All you need to do is think of the trials and tribulations of Wile E. Coyote from *The Road Runner* or Scratchy, the poor put upon cat, in The Itchy and Scratchy Show from *The Simpsons*.

The essential questions are then whether the difference between 'pathetic' and 'tragic' is one of degree or the scale of suffering or how we, the audience, respond to this. For Miller the key to the tragic is not how much the central character suffers or the amount of suffering our scenario dramatises; the reason why Mr B's death is not tragic is because it does not have any moral dimension, does not generate any 'illumination of the ethical' does not portray 'the human being in his struggle for happiness'. **Tragedy should evoke pity and generate sadness in the audience, but, according**

to **Miller, crucially it must also help us face the most difficult experiences in life, loss, injustice, suffering, cruelty, despair and ultimately death**. Tragedy must have profundity.

However, not everyone agrees that the common and literary meanings are distinct. Surveying the history of attempts at definition of the word 'tragedy', Terry Eagleton, for instance, comes to the conclusion that the only sustainable definition of a tragedy is a play that is 'very sad' and 'sometimes very very sad'. Certainly the action of tragedies always unleashes chaos and anarchy. **Whereas in comedies the release of mayhem is enjoyable in tragedies the impact is disturbing, destructive and profound**.

Aristotle's Tragedy

As Jennifer Wallace writes in *The Cambridge Introduction to Tragedy*, 'most of the questions about tragedy which continue to vex us today were first formulated by Aristotle'. We're going to limit ourselves to just a few of the key questions - about the nature of the protagonist, the cause of tragic action, the significance of plot and the emotional effect of tragedy on an audience.

(Though there's no requirement for you to use Aristotle's terminology in your exams, knowing at least some of these key terms is helpful and let's face it, impressive.)

In the seminal *The Poetics* Aristotle argued that the protagonist in a tragedy had to be high born and noble in rank or character. This was essential because, he argued, **a fall from a position of great power and status must have a catastrophic effect not just personally, but in terms of consequences for other characters as well as for society as a whole**. Moreover, a character's fall from the top to bottom of society, from King to pauper, is vertiginously steep and hence more awesome and dramatic.

The central protagonist was also important because the seeds of a tragedy were, for Aristotle, embedded in his character. Later critics have glossed **Aristotle's useful word 'hamartia' to mean a fatal, moral or tragic flaw in the protagonist's personality, such as moral blindness, naivety, ambition** and so forth. However, 'harmatia' seems to have originally had a narrower definition, referring to a terrible, erroneous decision a character makes. Generally, hamartia is used by critics in both senses. In *King Lear*, for instance, Lear's hamartia could be identified psychologically as his inability to distinguish appearance from reality and/or in terms of a calamitous decision he makes that sets the tragic action running, such as his foolish splitting of the kingdom between his daughters.

So, for Aristotle, Mr. B's story quoted above could become tragic if, firstly, the central character was Prince, or King, B. Secondly the grand piano falling on his head must have been the inevitable consequence of his own erroneous earlier decisions (such as rather foolish placing a heavy piano hanging out of a window over a street through which he was about to walk).

If you've studied *King Lear* you will be able to anticipate some of the objections modern literary critics raise against the identification of the cause of a tragedy as a fatal mistake or single psychological flaw. In *King Lear,* for instance, is the fatal mistake the breaking up of the kingdom or the relinquishing of power, but not status? Or is it the love test the King devises for his daughters, or, perhaps, the banishment of Cordelia and/or Kent? **Moreover modern**  **critics are not convinced that there can be a single cause explaining** something as complex as a tragedy and even less convinced that this **single cause must lie in the nature or behaviour of the protagonist**. In fact for many modern critics and theorists the causes of tragedy are inherent in the foundations of society, in history, power and ideology.

Another important aspect of Aristotle's theory of tragedy is his emphasis on the need for a satisfying plot and structure. **Whereas in comedies the general pattern moves from disorder to order, the reverse is true of tragedies; order collapses into disorder.** A vital part of this structural pattern is the protagonist's journey towards some horrified realisation that the fates (and other characters) have been working against him. Aristotle uses the terms 'peripeteia' - a tragic turn of events - and 'anagnorisis' - a moment of revelation, or epiphany - to chart this epic journey. Think, for example, of Othello's discovery that Iago has betrayed him (the peripeteia) and his sudden realisation that his wife, Desdemona, was entirely innocent (the anagnorisis).

The idea of 'catharsis' has also been both highly influential and as hotly contested. Catharsis refers to the effect of witnessing a tragedy on an audience. **According to Aristotle, witnessing characters' suffering in a tragic play leads to a cathartic purging or washing of the audience's emotions, so that we feel curiously uplifted and relieved at the end of the spectacle.** Consider this the next time you troop out of a theatre having watched *Hamlet* or when you finish the last page of *Tess of the D'Urbervilles*. Do you/did you just feel sadness? Or did you feel something else greater, more uplifting, something profound?

Other Critics & Theorists
A general consensus has formed that conflict lies at the heart of the tragic genre. But the focus on the cause of this conflict has shifted from the close up of the protagonist's actions (or mind) to a wider panoramic perspective of the whole society, from the internal to the external, from the individual to the societal, and back again over time. Two philosophers, Hegel and Nietzsche, developed influential and contrasting theories of tragedy which neatly illustrate these different foci.

<u>Hegel's Theory of Tragedy</u>

Two key ideas underpin the rationalist philosopher, Hegel's theory of tragedy:

- tragedies follow the same recognisable pattern as History
- the conflict in tragedies is not between good and evil, right and wrong, but between opposing ideologies.

Hegel believed there was a constant cyclical pattern to History: one set of ideas (a thesis) came in time to be challenged by a counter set of ideas (an antithesis). Eventually this clash of ideologies led to a better formulation of ideas - a synthesis. The same pattern could be mapped, he argued, onto tragedies. As in History, in tragedies, clear causes could therefore be identified, a sequence of events outlined, consequences measured and analysed, ideological debates weighed and evaluated.

Rejecting the notion that tragedies dramatise a battle between moral good and moral evil, between a noble tragic hero (think of Othello) and a villainous antagonist (think Iago) Hegel argued the agon, or conflict, was between what he called 'equally justified powers'. The ideas dramatised in tragedies were not good ones against bad, in either the moral or practical sense; **tragedies dramatised instead the conflict between competing, but equally understandable, value and belief systems**. Read through Hegelian tragic theory, the conflict between Othello and Iago, or Lear and his daughters, is between an old-fashioned essentially feudal ideology and an emerging more modern, individualistic and meritocratic one.

Tragedy, for Hegel, was all about the battle of ideas. Controversially, this rational theory of tragedy downplayed the audience's empathetic emotional reaction to characters' suffering. **Suffering of individual characters was, for Hegel, an unfortunate, but inevitable consequence of the onward march of ideas and of History**. His conviction that tragedies (and History) move forward progressively towards the re-establishment of eternal justice and divine order provided a justification for this suffering. Unsurprisingly other theorists, such as Nietzsche, found Hegel's theory both inadequate and morally unpalatable.

Nietzsche's Theory of Tragedy

Though, like Hegel, Nietzsche argued conflict is the essence of tragedy, he relocated the conflict within human nature itself. Human behaviour, according to Nietzsche, is not governed just by the brain - by Hegel's bloodless logic and rationality: we're far messier beings than that (you know he's right). Our reason is constantly embattled by more primal, anarchic and destructive energies within us. Drawing on Greek culture, Nietzsche labelled the rational, orderly  principle the 'Apollonian' and our wild, atavistic compulsions the 'Dionysiac'.

The structure of tragedies, **for Nietzsche, does not follow that of a civilised intellectual debate arriving at a reasoned conclusion. Instead they trace a violent overthrow; Apollonian selves crack open and the Dionysiac emerges bloodily from the ruins**. (If you are familiar with Freudian theory, you may recognise some kinship here with the idea of the Ego and the Id.) Obviously this usurpation does not take place in a measured, civilised or conscious way: wild abandon, crazy ecstasy, giddy intoxication, frenzy are unleashed by the triumph of the primitive, irrational Dionysiac. Think, for instance, of King Lear on the heath, as the storm rages, wildly stripping off his royal regalia.

Nietzsche also rejected Hegel's notion that tragedies end in the restoration of divine justice. Indeed he believed the opposite: the bleak conclusions of plays such as *Hamlet* and *King Lear* help us to face the implications of nihilism, i.e. the lack of divine justice presiding over our human affairs.

A.C. Bradley

The arguments over the central causes of tragedies are also illustrated by the work of the very influential Shakespeare scholar A.C. Bradley. In his lectures of 1904, Bradley put a new psychological spin on Aristotle's notion of the tragic hero's hamartia, proposing that **each of the great tragic heroes has a single recognisable tragic flaw. And according to Bradley, this tragic flaw was far more significant than external factors as the cause of tragedy**. Bradley also disagreed with Hegel, suggesting that though there was an ideological struggle at the heart of each tragedy, one side of this struggle was always more moral than the other.

Being philosophers interested primarily in ideas, Nietzsche and Hegel were not so much bothered by more technical elements of tragedies that, nevertheless, contribute significantly to the power of texts in performance. To argue, for instance, that it is the conflict or ideas, or in human nature, that makes Shakespeare's great tragedies great is to ignore the genius of Shakespeare's use of language. Any examination of a tragedy must explore philosophical questions of agency – who or what makes the tragedy happen, of course. But, for English Literature critics and students (and examiners), **the power of the experience of tragedy must lie to some extent in the complex dynamics of dialogue, the revelation of psyche through soliloquies, the capacity for language and action to move and involve us emotionally** as well as the experience of the text within a theatrical context. As English students, we know that language is the key to understanding ideas in literary texts and we are always interested in technique as well as themes, and most especially how these two aspects of texts are interrelated. In short, your own study of tragedy must embrace both the philosophical and artistic dimensions.

Comedy

This section will look briefly at what the prerequisites of comedies are, the various comic devices employed in drama and also a quick overview of the social function of comedy.

Comedies must be characterised by one thing alone: laughter. If this fails to happen then the proposed comedy has become a tragic failure. Analysing comedy is a difficult process for some of us. **Like explaining a joke to someone who doesn't get it, the enjoyment can suddenly be lost when**

dissecting the mechanisms that deliver uproarious enjoyment. E. B. White states that "analysing comedy is like dissecting a frog. Few people are interested and the frog dies of it." However, just as one must reject emotional responses to literature, it is important that you learn to identify different types of humour at play in comedies and become proficient at explaining how they generate laughter in the audience.

From a more general structural viewpoint, tragedy and comedy are united by their adherence to the age old narrative schema of Stasis – Complication – Crisis – Climax – Resolution. However, at each point the audience reactions must be vastly different. The resolution, in particular, will always be different. **Lord Byron claims that "all tragedies are finish'd by a death, all comedies are ended by a marriage."** While this happy ending of marriage may seem a little old-fashioned to the 21st Century cynic, you get the general idea. The play must end with a feeling of progression to better things; whether that be marriage, a new relationship, the realisation of a dream come true or just a general increase in happiness for the protagonist. Of course one character's happiness may be another character's unhappiness but generally we are encouraged to side with the comic hero and his/her antagonists must cheer them on with a frozen grin. Elder Olson describes this feelgood ending as similar to the tragic catharsis; both involving the purging of audience emotion. Olson calls this **katastasis** in comedy: the "restoration of the mind to a pleasant, or euphoric, condition of freedom from desires and emotions; conversion of the grounds of concern into nothing."

So if katastasis is our intended endpoint what happens in between? A lot of mayhem, to be honest. **Comedies revel in upturning the normal world, in creating confusion from ridiculous versions of the everyday or a trivialisation of the profound.** Inversion of normal power relations is common with the standard social superior shown to be substantially intellectually inferior to his social inferiors. Comedy is seen to reject the order that governs everyday life. However, unlike in tragedy, this overwhelming of order is seen as a bracing and liberating alternative to the stultifying order imposed by social norms. This type of comic disorder extends from the micro to the macro, from isolated event to philosophy as Eric Idle of Mony Python claims: "life doesn't make any sense, and we all pretend it does. Comedy's job is to point out that it doesn't make sense, and that it doesn't make much difference anyway."

This sense of the enjoyable chaos and anarchy of life as captured through comedy is created on a number of levels. Oscar Wilde's comedy of manners, *The Importance of Being Earnest*, is used here to exemplify some of these concepts.

1. Character:
    - Usually **limited stereotypes or stock characters** characterised by a comedy inducing flaw or behaviour. Normally, these character types are instantly recognisable to audiences. In satire their flaws are more representative of social values that need correction. Lady Bracknell's domineering matriarch or Jack's suave hypocrite or Cecily's ingénue are all classic examples.
    - Such characters' **values are usually wrong** as they prioritise the trivial and trivialise the important. Algy is the epitome of this where Wilde proposes him as a refreshingly honest pleasure seeker who runs counter to the stuffy Victorian morality Wilde attacks.
    - **Unusually stupid or unexpectedly clever**; usually relating to an inversion of social rank. Wilde draws upon an entire dramatic tradition of servants who are smarter or better men than their masters in his play.

2. Action:

- **Overall comedies progress from disorder and chaos to order and calm**: Jack finds his real identity and marries the girl he loves.

- Farce: the plot is full of **ridiculous situations** that don't happen normally: Jack being found in a cloakroom in Victoria Station.

- Character actions tend to the **incongruous or ridiculous**. Like in modern horror films, the characters do things that normal people would never do: Cecily's alternative fantasy life as recorded in her diary.

- Burlesque: before images of Dita von Teese and *Moulin Rouge* jump into your mind this is a different type of burlesque. In comedy this simply means creating comic anarchy by bestowing **mock dignity on trivialities and trivialising serious, lofty or profound things**. The whole of Wilde's play basically achieves this by promoting silliness and deprioritising earnestness.

- Usually contains a **clash between the generations** i.e. young and old grappling for superiority. Lady Bracknell versus everybody else in the play.

- In Romantic Comedies, the plot revolves around how **a certain pair navigate comically the obstacles thrown in their way as they seek love and fulfilment**; in this case the trials and tribulations that Jack must face to win Gwendolyn's hand.

- Will involve moments of **slapstick or purely physical comedy characterised by boisterous action, broad farce and horseplay**. Jack chasing Algy around his apartment demanding his cigarette case back or Jack's grand melancholy entrance in full Victorian mourning garb.

- **Unexpected [or sometimes quite expected] role reversals**: the most notable one of these is when the villain gets trapped in a trap of their own making. Algy's use of Jack's fictional brother Ernest to gain access to Cecily.

- Dramatic Irony: **where the audience is more fully aware of**

the situation than the overly confident character. We know that neither Jack or Algy are called Ernest as their beloveds proclaim the god-like power of that divine name.

- Irony: **the intended outcomes desired by a character are denied and the exact opposite occurs.** In this case Jack pretends to be Ernest in an elaborate deception when in fact he really was Ernest all along.

- **The villains of the play get their comeuppance and are justly punished** but depending upon the satirical nature of the drama sometimes forgiven. A classic example is the famous screen scene in R.B. Sheridan's *The School for Scandal*. Here the villain Joseph Surface, a supposed moral man, sees his web of lies and deceptions literally exposed by the falling of a screen. Said screen reveals Lady Teazle to her husband, Sir Peter, who has been listening to all types of two-faced outpourings from Joseph and he realises the true villain that lies behind the moral sentiments Joseph is so fond of reciting.

- **The play ends happily**. All the pairings are to be married: Jack and Gwendolen; Algy and Cecily; Chasuble and Prism; Lady Bracknell is satisfied, for a little while, at least!

3. Dialogue

Here playwrights can employ a dizzying array of weapons by which to generate humour such as

- Jokes: you know what these are!

- Puns: **humorous play on words** that have the same sounds [homophones] but different meanings. The most famous example is the final line of *The Importance of Being Earnest*.

- Sarcasm: **withering putdowns** that signify the superiority of a character over another.

- Irony: **where a character confidently asserts something that is completely at odds with their character and actions**: Gwendonlen's strident claim that she is "never wrong". In satire it is used to expose hypocrisy.

- Asides: a **conspiratorial communication between a character and the audience** that is highly artificial. It usually engineers delicious dramatic irony and reveals the discrepancy between what is said and what is thought. A modern equivalent is the use of internal dialogue in *Peep Show*.

- Freudian Slips: like an aside only that the **character simultaneously reveals their true intentions to both audience and characters on stage**. Usually this is associated with someone trying to keep their real intentions hidden. Jack's crucial slip when he proclaims "Gwendolen, I must get christened at once – I mean we must get married at once. There is no time to be lost."

- Repartee: **rapid-fire verbal jousting between two characters** as they wrestle for superiority. See Jack and Algy's bickering after Gwendolen and Cecily realise neither of them are called Ernest.

- Wit: a **verbal flair** that establishes a comic hero's credentials. To quote Alexander Pope: that which "oft was thought, but ne'er so well exprest." Wilde's play is packed with witticisms such as "All women become like their mothers. That is their tragedy. No man does. That's his."

- Malapropisms: **a clownish misuse of language under the guise of being a master of expression**. The most famous example will be discussed later in our discussion of critical theory where we discuss Sheridan's *The Rivals*. His character Mrs. Malaprop epitomises a type of intellectual vanity that is undermined every time she opens her mouth.

Comedy can also be sourced extratextually through the medium of parody. **Parody is a humorous or satirical imitation of a serious piece of literature or writing and can be very funny**. However, for parody to be effective the audience must be fully aware of the source text or parody target

that is being mocked; without this recognition the parody flatlines. Classic examples are drawing upon vampire literature or the mad scientist from James Whales' 1931 film version of *Frankenstein* in new irreverent ways that eradicate the terror and replace it with silly but recognisable echoes. See Graham Linehan's *Black Books* for a brilliant parody of the mad scientist. A more obvious example would be Mike Myer's Austin Powers films, which parody the James Bond spy genre. A famous literary example is Alexander Pope's mock epic *The Rape of the Lock* from 1717, which trivialised brilliantly the tradition of great Greek and Roman epic narratives from Homer to Virgil. In Wilde's play he parodies the suspense-filled detective fiction so popular in his day (thanks to Sir Arthur Conan Doyle's *Sherlock Holmes*). The mystery of solving Jack's origins and Miss Prism's prime suspect role in the death of a three volume novel are told with a white-knuckle suspense they definitely don't merit – hence why it's so funny.

The nature of the laughter produced is very important to take into account when studying comedies: are we laughing *at* or *with* the characters? This decides the taste left in our mouths once katastasis has finished and such considerations lead us into the social function of comedy. Why do we laugh at what the playwright instructs us to laugh at? Albert Cook argues that **"comedy is approval not disapproval, of present society; it is conservative, not liberal."** In this case we are always laughing at the characters and the comedy we experience becomes a "sort of social gesture. By the fear which it inspires it restrains eccentricity: it pursues a utilitarian aim of general improvement," according to Henri Bergson. In this case sympathy, which is a necessity for tragedy, must be banished; the audience must not care one jot about the characters they laugh at. Andrew Stott describes this as the "cruelty of comedy, which involves a certain degree of desensitisation, **allows us to stand back and look upon human misfortune from an emotional distance, sometimes even deriving great pleasure from it.**"

The counter-argument to this cruel comic quashing of individual eccentricities is that it is not conservative at all; rather it is radical and transformative. By presenting a ridiculous version of reality satirical comedies can force us to interrogate our own personal values and the values of the society we are part of. In this scenario comedy becomes morally transformative and a vehicle for social change through the recalibration of widely held social values. **Satires identify and punish figures of vice and immorality through scathing and unrelenting ridicule**. In this case you need to ask yourself what aspects of society or social behaviour the play is attacking. In satire the characters

or behaviours exposed will always be social in some way. The character's fault cannot be attributed to purely individual oddness; if so then the comedy has strayed into conservative correction and social stagnation rather than social change. **Another aspect that must be acknowledged with regard to satire is that it need not be comic**. Many a scathing satire has been completely devoid of humour; see George Orwell's *Nineteen Eighty-four*. Even when satire chooses a comic exterior "there is always a dark edge to the laughter. Whether to heal or correct, or to punish, the satirist is always preoccupied with the exposure of vice and error" [Hannah Lavery].

Now that you have a firm grasp on the notable characteristics of both tragedy and comedy, which allows you to confidently discuss genre, you must also remember that contextual factors will be equally important. While the more general contextual factors of biographical and socio-historical factors will get a more intense workout in Chapter 20, you must possess a strong awareness of the intricacies of dramatic context.

Dramatic Context

It may seem obvious, but **you need to display the same sort of awareness of genre and context as expected with prose**. Can you tell the difference between Greek tragedy and Shakespearean tragedy? If so why are they different? Where did Georgian sentimental comedy hide the ferocious satirical teeth of Restoration comedy...and why? How is Luigi Pirandello's modernist surrealism different to Henrik Ibsen's naturalism? What does it mean when someone calls your staging of a key scene from *King Lear* Brechtian? Is there a link between Samuel Beckett's tragicomedy *Waiting for Godot* and Tom Stoppard's postmodernist *Rosencrantz and Guildenstern are Dead*? Is the theatre of cruelty as interesting as it sounds? Who knows? You must! Displaying a keen awareness of dramatic context and the expected conventions of genre establishes your expertise and tells the examiner that they are in safe hands for the rest of your essay. If you can display an awareness of the dramatic conventions of these various genres and the social conditions that produced and demanded them then your analysis will be greatly improved.

Such nuanced awareness of intratextual, extratextual and contextual factors will be a key element of any comparative essay, especially where the contextual factors of the texts contrast greatly. The next chapter explores how to attack the tricky obstacle course of the comparative essay – a messy drama for sure.

16. Comparative Essays

The title gives it away here really - comparative essays want you to display not only your ability to intelligently talk about literary texts but also your ability to make meaningful connections between them. Exam boards will heavily prioritise the AO4 aspects of your essay here. **Comparative essay writing is probably the most challenging type of literary discussion you will undertake,** but, as shown with the previous types of literary analysis, there is also a method to this particular madness. **The most important step is to plan well**. Roughly speaking 80% of your time will be given over to reading [texts, critical responses, context], note-making mind-mapping, link-making and paragraph planning, aka good old fashioned thinking, while 20% will be given over to writing the essay itself.

The most important job for you as an essay writer is to find the substantial linking topic between your chosen texts. In some cases you will be given a question that provides this for you, but the most challenging, and in our opinion the most rewarding, road is the one you follow yourself. And unfortunately you can blame no one but yourself if it leads to undesirable locations i.e. acute mental breakdown, the bottom of a cliff or cardiac arrest! Fundamentally, your topic must allow you to produce meaningful discussion where you can talk about both texts together.

The first starting point is your **topic**. This **must be broad enough to allow substantial thematic overlapping of the texts**. However, too little overlap and it will be difficult to connect the texts; too much overlap and your discussion will be lopsided and one-dimensional.

To think about it visually, you don't want Option A below [not enough overlap] or Option B [two much overlap]. You want Option C. This option allows substantial common links to be built between your chosen texts where discussion arises from both fundamental similarities AND differences.

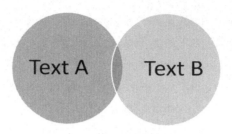

Option A: too many differences

Option B: too many similarities

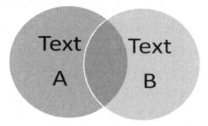

Option C: suitable number of similarities and differences

This final option will generate the most interesting discussion as it will allow substantial similarities to emerge as well as differences. Obviously, this principle applies for three texts and upwards, which is a very challenging comparative exercise. The best comparative essays actually find that what seemed like clear similarities become subtle differences and vice versa while still managing to find rock solid similarities to build their foundations on.

An example would be useful at this stage. A student studying Pat Barker's *Regeneration* and Roddy Doyle's *The Woman Who Walked Into Doors* might easily decide that the topics of gender or trauma would be a broad enough starting point. And they would be right. If they decided that the topic of food and drink was suitable they would begin to struggle. While certainly food and drink are present in both texts they are not thematically important to either. Clearly the topics of gender and trauma are much more meaningfully relevant to both.

Once you have chosen your topic your focus must narrow to find a suitable **question**. Often this can come from thinking about your **argument**, which is another narrowing down process. Your argument is essentially what an extended opinion or observation about your chosen topic. What is it you actually have to say about the topic as presented in the two texts? If you have some idea of what your argument is you simply tailor your question to suit the argument. However, be warned - when you start writing your argument may begin to refine itself as your respond to your initial ideas. This is no bad thing. **If your argument does shapeshift as you write go back to the start and refine it from the beginning or account for the refinement of your argument in your conclusion.** This way your argument is consistent and you are developing it as you write - a sign of an excellent literature student. Starting with one argument and ending with a slightly different one should be seen as a strength rather than a weakness - embrace it.

In general the process of answering a comparative question will look something like the following diagram:

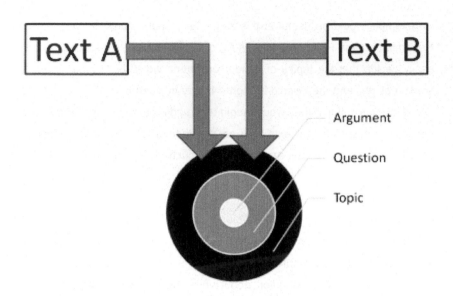

Again, continuing our example of *Regeneration* and *The Woman Who Walked Into Doors* from before this process may end up looking like this:

Topic	**Gender** ***Trauma***
Question	**How is the impact of gender stereotypes on the individual explored in the two texts?** ***Explore how the treatment of trauma is presented in the two texts.***
Argument	**In *The Woman Who Walked Into Doors* adherence to gender stereotypes impacts negatively on females but positively on males; in *Regeneration* deviation from stereotypes impacts negatively on males but positively on females.** ***The treatment of trauma in both texts is determined by the social class status of the sufferer, which determines how successfully trauma is resolved.***

Once this process has been completed then it is down to the fine detail of making connections between your chosen texts, a process that must entail a lot of note-making and mindmapping etc. Once this has been done then you need to take the raw material of your planning and refine it into an essay plan.

Consider the following structures. Which one is best and why?

Essay Structure #1

1. Introduction
2. Main body paragraph #1 - Text A
3. Main body paragraph #2 - Text A
4. Main body paragraph #3 - Text B
5. Main body paragraph #4 - Text B
6. Conclusion

Essay Structure #2

1. Introduction
2. Main body paragraph #1 - Text A
3. Main body paragraph #2 - Text A
4. Main body paragraph #3 - Text B
5. Main body paragraph #4 - Text B
6. Comparison of main body paragraphs #1 & #3 - Text A + B
7. Comparison of main body paragraphs #2 & #4 - Text A + B
8. Conclusion

Essay Structure #3

1. Introduction
2. Main body paragraph #1 - Text A + B
3. Main body paragraph #2 - Text A + B
4. Main body paragraph #3 - Text A + B
5. Main body paragraph #4 - Text A+ B
6. Conclusion

We hope you will find that option 3 is most desirable. Option 1 is the dreaded 'here is everything I know about text A, followed by everything I know by Text B' approach where the examiner has to work out what the connections are between the texts. This will score the lowest marks. Option 2 is better as there is some attempt to compare the two texts. However, it is a very inefficient way of comparing the two texts. **For comparative essay writing the most important thing is to discuss both texts together. This is the most effective and efficient way of achieving your overall aim**. Option 3 does this by comparing and contrasting the two texts under common umbrella headings. This naturally encourages comparison.

For our chosen example one such paragraph heading could be 'coping mechanisms for trauma' which would reveal that Paula Spencer in *The Woman Who Walked Into Doors* is denied access to medical treatment because she is a working class woman, whereas the upper class male officers in *Regeneration* have full access to such treatment. However, an interesting common result is that both sufferers are retraumatised [Paula continues to suffer domestic abuse in silence while the officers are sent back to the front to the site of their original trauma].

Regardless of what texts you choose, the most important work is always at the planning stage. Once your focus is approximately right the rest of the essay falls into place. If you find you are running out of discussion you probably need to widen the range of your question. Conversely, if you discover you have not reached the great analysis you planned and you are already near the word limit then your question needs to narrow its focus. **It is a trial and error process, but a process that becomes easier with practice**. You begin to get a feel for what the right type of question will be. Ultimately, always follow your intellectual interests. Determine what you have to say about the two texts and work backwards if you need to.

The following example of well-handled comparison comes from an AS coursework essay exploring the presentation of gender roles in Pat Barker's *Regeneration* and *The Road* by Cormac McCarthy:

> As part of their exploration of gender roles both McCarthy and Barker examine the effects that the breakdown of traditional gender roles has on the 'weaker' characters in both novels. Yealland, the doctor who Rivers visits towards the end of the book has a particularly aggressive,

masculine method for dealing with 'shell-shocked' patients; he uses electro-shock therapy until the patient's physical symptoms are alleviated but does nothing to comfort the patient emotionally. This overly masculine style works to some degree; in the case of Callan, his mutism is cured. However, the sheer discomfort caused by the electro-shock process itself does nothing but add to his emotional trauma. This method is diametrically opposed to Rivers' intimate 'mother-like' method in which he offers comfort to, and fulfils the emotional needs of the patient. This can be seen in the way that he deals with any of his patients but a clear example would be the manner in which he breaks down Prior's overly-masculine emotional wall by asking him questions such as 'Did you get back to sleep' and telling him that 'we all care about what the people around us think, whether we admit it or not.' However, while this method certainly seems to be more effective in comforting the traumatised patients than Yealland's violent approach, Rivers is still incapable of curing those suffering from the most severe cases of trauma such as Burns – when he goes to visit Burns while on leave, Rivers sees that he still has trouble eating and sleeping just as he did when he was at Craiglockhart. This sense of emotional comfort being impossible in the most severe cases is taken and emphasised to a much greater extent when looking at The Man and The Boy in The Road. *Despite the fact that The Man successfully takes on both a maternal and paternal role for the Boy by protecting him physically and emotionally, he is still ultimately powerless to help him.*

This sense of powerlessness could be seen as a reflection of the 9/11 attacks, which took place in America five years before the publication of The Road, in which thousands of people were forced to watch the planes crash into the towers with no way of stopping them. Cormac McCarthy emphasises this point through The Man's death at the very end of the novel. It would appear then, that regardless of how successfully an authoritative figure fulfils a combination of motherly and fatherly roles, if the situation is extreme and traumatic enough, the 'victim' will be beyond help ; as stated by Michelle Balaev 'Traumatic

179

experience is understood as a fixed and timeless photographic negative stored in an un-locatable place of the brain.' Both writers would seem to suggest, therefore, that the damage done to powerless, innocent individuals by corrupt social structures cannot be healed.

Notice how the first paragraph begins with a clear topic sentence which both texts brought together. The four or five sentences that follow examine the topic in *Regeneration*. A short phrase operates as a comparative discourse marker to clearly signal the switch to *The Road*: 'to a much greater extent'. The comparison here is a dissimilarity between the texts, illustrating the fact that underneath the surface similarity of both texts exploring the same topic there is a significant contrast. A further four sentences substantiate this point before the second paragraph concludes by neatly bringing the texts together in a summative conclusion about what they appear to have in common.

17. Re-creative Writing

<u>Why write a re-creative piece?</u>
Watch professionals play music or sport and it can look pretty straightforward. Until you have a go yourself. Watch some cricket on TV and some guy runs in and flings a ball at another guy with a big stick who simply has to hit it. How difficult can that be? As we know from our greatest writers, suffering can be instructive. Strap on some batting pads and get a bowling machine to bowl a small hard red projectile at you at over 80 mph. We reckon you'll come to a different, more informed opinion rather quickly.

Seemingly effortless performance actually requires great skill, effort, stamina, as well as hours of practice and training. We all know it's easy to sit on the sidelines and criticise. Having a go yourself usually results in greater respect for the musician/ sportsperson/ painter. The same is true with great writing. **The re-creative response offered by some exam boards makes you think like a writer, places you inside the writer's skin, forces you to make the same sorts of decisions about narration, plot, language, dialogue, characterisation as the writer.** Think of climbing inside a text as being like climbing into a formula one racing car or a fighter jet. The experience should be exciting and little bit scary. Look at all those controls!

Certainly the experience should challenge you. But it will also refine your appreciation of writers' skills. As well as improving your reading, it may also improve your own writing. Writing in someone else's style inevitably makes you notice and reflect upon your own. If there are things you especially like about the way someone writes you can use this as guidance for your own writing.

Re-creative writing is defined as a new piece of writing based on the style and features of a source text. If you are studying a collection of poems, for instance, you could write a new one, preferably to fit at a particular point in the collection. An extra chapter from a novel or scene from a play would also fulfil the criteria. Perhaps a more interesting approach, however, is to prise open a gap in the source text and write into this.

In Ian McEwan's novel *Enduring Love* the opening chapter describes a traumatic experience that triggers the plot. This experience is narrated by the protagonist, Joe Rose, beginning from the point at which he and his girl friend, Clarissa, sit down in a field to enjoy a nice picnic. A small, seemingly insignificant detail in this opening refers to an important, but minor character, John Logan, whose car is found parked at the scene with its doors open.

Switching narrative point of view would allow us to retell the story through the perspective of John Logan. Perhaps we could start a little earlier than McEwan does, with Logan driving happily, or unhappily, in his car. (Logan will end up dangling from a rope attached to a balloon rising high up into the clear sky.) Perhaps we could write the thoughts racing through his mind as he races towards his doom.

In every novel, play or film scenes follow some characters, whilst other characters remain 'off-stage' or just hover in the background. What is Othello doing, for instance, while Iago entertains the audience with his soliloquies? Some scenes are reported rather than fully dramatised, providing further opportunities. **Every novel, play or film thus has a shadow version of off-stage action, character and plot development. This shadow is a rich source of material for re-creative writing**.

How might we make a piece of re-creative writing convincing? Remember you are going to be trying to write like a professional novelist, poet or playwright, probably one with a substantial literary reputation. In other words these people are highly skilled writers, so you're going to have to be on your mettle. Firstly it's vital that the characters behave, speak, move and think in ways that are consistent with how they appear in the source text. Your narrative style also has to accurately mimic the original. If there's a talkative omniscient narrator, or if the narrator makes minimal interventions in the story, if the playwright uses extensive stage directions or none, you must follow. If you deviate, then you need a very good reason which you'd explain in your accompanying critical commentary. **The commentary is, in effect, a short critical essay, analysing the source in relation to your re-creative response**.

So, before you begin writing you need to analyse the source material just as closely, if not more closely, than you would if you were writing an analytical essay on it. Impressionists spend hours studying those they impersonate. You will need to devote a similar level of attention to your source text.

This won't just be an interesting process in itself, nor will in only pay dividends in terms of your re-creative writing; it will also be extremely beneficial for your commentary. Each exam board recommends a different balance between the re-creative piece and its commentary. Usually at least as many, if not more, marks will be awarded to the commentary. **Therefore at least as much effort needs to go in to the commentary as in to the re-creative writing itself**.

Bearing in mind what we have said consistently in this book about over-reliance on essay formulas or models, we tentatively suggest the following guidelines for your commentary. You may, of course, wish to adapt this advice to suit yourself. In fact that is what we would really like you to do.

Commentary
   1. Introduction - key features of the source text - its themes, style, genre, structure, context and so forth.
   2. Close analysis of some of these key features, such as narrative technique and language.
   3. Explanation of how you have imitated these features, using examples from both the source and from your re-creative piece.
   4. Evaluation of your success.

If half or more of the marks are awarded for the commentary, why you might ask, bother to write a re-creative piece?

Well, in addition to what we said earlier about appreciation and challenge, **writing a re-creative piece will exercise your imagination**. This makes your brain healthy and happy (honestly!). We recommend you have a go at a few different pieces of re-creative writing, using as wide a range of writers as possible. To use two writers we've already referred to in this book, writing in the minimalist, masculine style of someone like Ernest Hemingway and then in the voluptuously decadent Gothic style of Angela Carter's *The Bloody Chamber* will push you to two stylistic extremes. (Short stories are particularly useful for re-creative tasks as they can provide a rich range of styles and themes.)

At GCSE level there is usually a number of opportunities for different types of writing. At A-level this sometimes shrinks to just the critical essay. While this is a very important form of response to a piece of literature, it's not the only one. Every production of a play, for example, is essentially a new creative response. **So, it's refreshing to be able to convey your response to literature in a different form at least once during the course**.

What about the marking? Isn't it less reliable, more a matter of taste, than the marking of regular essays? Certainly fears about the marking put some schools and students off doing the re-creative piece. But this is a false fear. **Coursework examiners really enjoy reading re-creative pieces and are well disposed to anything original and ambitious**. The commentary ensures that marks can be allocated accurately for analytical skill. In our experience the marks awarded to re-creative coursework are at least as good, if not generally higher, than for the more conventional coursework essays. Most exam boards also provide mark schemes and exemplar material.

The following example is a recreative piece written in response to Carter's *The Bloody Chamber* for AS coursework. After reading the first two thirds of the story, 'The Company of Wolves' (Carter's radical retellling of the fairy tale 'Little Red Riding Hood'), the students completed their own endings to the story, trying to stay as close as possible to Carter's elaborate prose style and true to her feminist thematic concerns. As we join the story the wolf has gobbled up grandmother and is waiting in her bed for the little girl in the red hood to arrive...

The Company of Wolves

Red Riding Hood knocked on her grandmother's front door:

"rat-a-tap-tap".

Hearing no answer, gingerly she pushed open the door and entered the house. Delicately she placed her boots by the door, well away from the face of the oil-burning stove.

How strange it was, she thought for grandmother not to answer and for the door to be unlocked. Perhaps she was out, or ill in bed. Up the stairs the young girl went, calling out before her 'grandmother, oh, grandmother'. At the top of the stairs and still no answer.

From the entrance to her bedroom Red Riding Hood could see that Grandmother was indeed still in bed, though it was now mid-morning.

'Grandmother?'

The closer Red Riding Hood drew, the more she noticed that her grandmother smelled somewhat oddly; a little musky, perhaps, as if she had just gobbled a rare steak.

"Grandmother, what are you doing in bed, are you not well?"

"No my dear, I'm perfectly fine, thank you." How rough and gruff her grandmother sounded. She must have a terribly sore throat.

Suddenly grandmother threw off the blankets and leaped out of the bed.

"Grandmother! You're going to break your old fragile bones moving so quickly," said the astonished young girl.

Rapidly grandmother ripped all her clothes off. When Red Riding Hood opened her eyes again a handsome young huntsman stood before her smiling. Off came another layer of clothes and last of all the handsome mask of the face. Red Riding Hood remained motionless for a moment staring at the wolf crouched in front of her slavering and snarling with vicious intent.

A moment later the ravenous wolf had pounced and gobbled the poor girl whole!

Now Red Riding Hood found herself inside his stomach. And a very dark and smelly place it was indeed. Quickly she whipped out her pen knife. Swiftly she sliced an incision into the wolf's stomach lining, through the skin to cut up along the outer fur. Poor wolfie let out a blood-curdling scream and fell flat on his back stone dead. Carefully Red Riding Hood widened the bloody hole. Such impressive speed and meticulousness - her mother would be proud. Stepping briskly from the gaping wound, brushing off the grisly, bloody entrails and half-digested unspeakable stuff, Red Riding Hood set busily to work cutting the wolf's head off. What hard graft it was with just a small penknife. And really, so much blood.

After decapitating the wolf, the young woman brewed the kettle and made herself an extra-large cup of tea accompanied with a hefty slice of grandmother's fruit cake. Her composure regained, she took the mobile out of her pinny. A few quick shots of her with the wolf's head and ping off they went to all her friends.

Though this is an entertaining piece of writing that reads as if it was fun to write, it was a first draft and needed redrafting before being submitted for coursework. If you know *The Bloody Chamber*, you will recognise a few lapses in the accuracy of the imitation. Even if you haven't read Carter's book, you may recall that it was written in 1979. While it's true that Carter deliberately uses anachronisms, such as a soldier on a bike from the 1st WW appearing in a vampire story, in 1979 people didn't have mobile phones. Nor could they upload photos to online social networks as neither technology existed...

That said, the candidate correctly predicts the sort of switch Carter makes in the storyline - the little girl avoids her predetermined fate as the victim of the wolf to be saved by a huntsman. Instead she saves herself with impressively unflappable sangfroid. Small details are not quite right, however, showing that the reading of the source material has not been meticulous enough. In the original, for example, there are no stairs and therefore no upstairs bedroom - all the gory action takes place downstairs.

PART THE THIRD

CONTEXTS & CRITICS

PART THE THIRD: Contexts and Critics

18. Using Critics Effectively

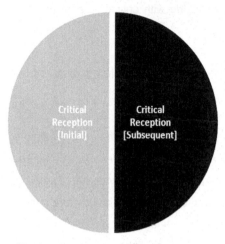

Possibly the major difference between GCSE literature study and A-Level literary study can be summed up in one word: **critics**. So what's the big deal with these critics? What are they and why are they so important? Well, unfortunately for the majority of English students most of their initial ideas about a literary text already exist in published form. Nowadays, critical responses to literary texts are as important as the original texts themselves. Critical responses present a hugely diverse range of engagement points with a text; they can be concerned with literary strategies employed or perhaps be interested in structural devices or maybe in thematic concerns or contextual factors or maybe even in theoretical explorations [more of this later].

But what does it mean to be a critic? In essence every literature essay is a piece of criticism, meaning that every English literature student is a critic in their own right. However, where GCSE essays are really personal responses in isolation, in a critical vacuum almost, A-level essays must be careful to survey the landscape of critical interpretations before mapping out their own interpretative journey through a text. It is important that students critique literary texts informed by what has gone before and can engage with criticism. On one hand this shows a well-rounded, three-dimensional response to the text; on the other hand, it also provides interesting opportunities for discussion by challenging other critical viewpoints. Critics can be used in a number of ways and to varying degrees of usefulness.

189

The most limited way to use a critic is simply to **name drop** them. This is usually the resort of the student who chances their arm by throwing in a well-known critic without really engaging with their ideas in any way. Unfortunately, such name-dropping will not get you many, if any, marks for **AO5**. Remember that old chestnut? Here's a quick refresher. AO5 is the aspect of your essay concerned with engaging with critical responses to the text.

Consider the following examples and try to rate them in terms of which one uses a critic most effectively.

1. *Alexander Pope's* The Rape of the Lock *presents the behaviour of aristocratic men and women in a satirical way. Ellen Pollak says that gender norms were not as they are today. In the poem the Baron and Belinda come across as silly people with too much money and time on their hands. Both genders are seen as badly behaved and in need of moral instruction, which Pope was only glad to deliver. He was trying to laugh two Catholic families back together after a trivial incident that showed how women could be treated as property to be taken at will.*

2. *Aleksander Pode's heroic poem* Rope of the Lake *was written in 1917, which was known as the Augustan times. In the play Belinda, who is really Arabella Fermor, is assaulted by the Baron, who actually died of small-pox after the hair was stolen anyway. The play is full of gender conflict in that both genders are in conflict throughout the poem. The ladies are shown to be fiery and fierce while the men are shown to be weak and sneaky. Ellen Pollak says that there was a "myth of passive womanhood."*

3. *Pope's poem was written in 1711, then revised in 1714 and again in 1717. The story of the poem is all about how Baron, Lord Petre seized a curl of Arabella Fermor without permission. The two families fell out as a result and Pope was asked to laugh them together again. Time and time again, Pope shows both genders to be foolish, selfish and*

trivial - anything but heroic or noble, which is what is normal for the epic poetry so revered at the time. Still a very patriarchal society the Augustans proscribed very limited social roles for women. Ellen Pollak describes this as the "myth of passive womanhood." Essentially she means that women were supposed to be passive and silent and really seen but not heard. In the poem this is true as Belinda suffers at the hands of a male, the Baron.

4. Alexander Pope's mock-heroic poem, written in 1717, is a satirical presentation of Augustan gender norms. However, given the  patriarchal society that Pope came from and the associated views of women as inferior, the poem can be seen to still prioritise male dominance. Despite the clear case of male violence against women in the poem along with the debatable punishment of such behaviour, women are presented as fundamentally more ridiculous in a world full of ridiculous figures. Belinda's role as victim is undermined by her own transgressive behaviour; she is a very masculine female in the poem. Ellen Pollak proposes "the myth of passive womanhood" to explain how female subservience to males was naturalised at this time (Human Sexuality, 153). It is Belinda's refusal to adhere to this subservient passivity that results in her symbolic social punishment in the poem. However, Pope's poem also allows Belinda a rare opportunity of female power. She dominates the poem completely and thus is a refreshing antidote to the weak, limited females found in much contemporary literature. Pollak's concept is therefore relevant by its complete absence, almost

as if Pope shows what females should be by presenting their opposite in an ambiguous light.

We hope you will find that they increase in quality towards the end. **Example 1** is not bad as it displays some knowledge of the poem and the context and even displays some knowledge of an important critic. However, it is clear that they cannot remember exactly what Pollak says about Augustan gender norms and they ascribe such a sweeping, obvious generalisation to her that it is almost redundant. **Example two** is horror writing but not in the intentional Gothic sense; it's riddled with errors of an embarrassing variety i.e. mistaking a poem for a play, misspelling the author's name. It also pulls off an old classic trick, which we call the 'critical hit-and-run.' This essentially involves throwing a critic in to prove your point but failing to explain how it reinforces your discussion in any way. To be fair, it does show knowledge of a critic, but the critic seems to be used in a contradictory way. Without any subsequent discussion, the critical quotation simply hangs limply at the end of the paragraph contributing very little.

Example three is much better and is quite astute in terms of social context. It actually quotes Pollak and her theory and goes on to explain it, thus showing sound engagement with the critic. However, it is not used productively as Pollak's theory actually contradicts the action of the poem. Belinda is not a stereotypical, passive female at all and this lack of correlation between poem and critical concept is not recognised. We are getting there. Hopefully, you will agree that **example four** is the best. Well, it is; and for a number of reasons. Firstly, it has a clear argument at the beginning about the poem satirising gender norms. It also uses social context sparingly but very effectively. Finally, the use of Pollak is intelligently realised [and properly referenced, we hope you've noticed!] by engaging with the actual concept. The essay recognises what this term implies as well as acknowledging that Belinda does not adhere to it and why Pope would not want her to. It also contributes to the previously stated argument of Pope's poem as a comment on gender norms.

So, it is clear, we hope, that using critics in your essays will be very productive in helping you generate the best discussion possible. However, this does lead to the temptation to over rely on critics leading to essays that are not much more that elaborate **critical surveys** of a text. Critics really should only be used where they benefit discussion rather than just for the sake of it. Again, to look at the case of Pope's *The Rape of the Lock*, there is a substantial amount of critical material related to the text. Let's say you decide to tackle a question from section B of OCR's F663 exam paper; let's go for a classic example:

"For women, sex is a means to an end, for men it is an end in itself"
In light of this view, consider ways in which writers explore differing attitudes
to sex.

Immediately it should be obvious that the topic is gender focused and will require an exploration of critics who have pondered this aspect of the poem. You will probably need to think about Ellen Pollak's aforementioned myth of passive womanhood, Valerie Rumbold's argument that Belinda is the most virile figure in the poem, Christa Knellwolf's discussion of how Belinda's simultaneous sympathetic and censuring treatment reflects  patriarchal anxieties about women or Sheila Delany's view that female beauty's function is ultimately to catch a husband, no more than this. You would, however, be advised to stay away from Howard Erskine-Hill's political readings of Catholic-Protestant tension in the poem or Laura Brown's view of Belinda as embodying the violence of colonial exploitation. As fascinating as these sound, they are not essential to the topic at hand and will dilute rather than concentrate the power of your discussion. **Make sure that the critics you use are relevant to your topic**. Use them productively to help you explore and/or refine your argument about the topic.

The key word in the previous sentence was the possessive pronoun "your." Remember, a literature essay is your **own personal response** to a topic and you must ensure that it is so. You are bound to spot connections and details, no matter how small, that others have missed or simply not prioritised. Your essays must not become grotesque ventriloquist displays where you parrot the views of critics while providing the filler in between. To use a flight analogy, if your argument is your plane and is constructed robustly then the presence of critics in your essay acts as the runway that will ensure your trajectory soars to the heights of success. Conversely, unwieldy use of critics will clog up your essay and prevent take off. As stated previously, critics should only be cited where they are useful, positively impacting upon your discussion. If they fail to do this, or worse they lead to unnecessary digression, bin them.

High priests of truth

There is a temptation to view critics as high priests of truth, oracles who reveal absolute meaning for the unenlightened. This is quite an unhealthy attitude in literary study as well as in life. **Dispensers of truth must be interrogated rigorously, evaluated and stretched to find strengths and weaknesses in their argument.** As we explained in our introduction, literature study is "not about absolute knowledge; it is about opinions and ideas, values and feelings." You must forgive our own name-dropping here but, it is a valid point. Your opinion must stretch further than the original text; it must also encompass critical interpretations of the text.

When exploring the critical landscape it is natural to gather allies around us rather than challenging foes; using these critical fragments to shore against our ruins, like T. S. Eliot in *The Waste Land*. This is fertile material, of course, but there is substantial value to be gained from gathering those **dissonant voices** that you disagree with. Why? If you think about it, the critics you admire or the texts that you love instil a certain critical blindness. Admiration clouds weaknesses and your judgement becomes less objective. Often you will find that interrogating texts or critics that you fundamentally dislike/disagree with will reap more interesting results.

Engaging with a perspective you find offensive or ridiculous jolts you out of your intellectual comfort zone as you must argue, sometimes vociferously, with this grating viewpoint. Ultimately, it can open up areas of discussion you would never have considered and will enrich your discussion in a way that a sympathetic critic cannot. The former will make you work very hard to justify your own viewpoint whereas the latter will merely reinforce it. **It is more likely that a disagreeable critic will help you refine and strengthen your argument in a more productive way than an agreeable critic.** Just get acquainted with the French theorist Jean Baudrillard as an extreme example [see next section]. **Our recommendation is to try use at least one critic you disagree with in your essays.** This type of engagement shows an intellectual daring and confidence that is characteristic of the outstanding student.

But what can the outstanding student do if they are studying a text with little or no critical treatment? Will their AO5 marks be destined to be stalled on the runway, to languish at absolute zero forever? Not on our watch. This barren critical wasteland can be encountered, especially if you decide to write about literary texts that are very recent or quite obscure. In some ways this is an advantage as your essay will have the gleam of the unfamiliar by which you can dazzle your examiner. However, if desperate online detective work reaps no rewards then you will have to take the backdoor route.

We have argued that such an oblique approach can be useful in attacking the fortress of an essay question; it can also be extremely productive when thinking about critics. Examiners will see the same old critics associated with the same old texts all the time. **You can raise your essay above the hoi polloi by introducing an unusual new critical voice or opinion, or even using a familiar critic in new, unfamiliar contexts**. What is to stop you from applying Ellen Pollak's myth of passive womanhood to Richard Brinsley Sheridan's *The Rivals*? Belinda is a lot like Miss Lydia Languish: spoilt, conceited, vain, rich and dangerous due to her nonconformity. Pollak allows a discussion of how Lydia is socially dangerous and how Sheridan must ensure that she is assimilated back into Georgian social expectations in his syrupy happy ending.

Stretch it a little further by going back to John Brannigan's discussion of the temporary and ultimately debilitating effects of social freedom for women in Pat Barker's *Regeneration*. This can be applied to Lydia Languish too: the intensity of her romantic fantasy at the start of the play ultimately makes her disappointment at having to conform to reality at the end of the play all the sourer. Once you get going on this train of thought, there is no stopping you.

If there are no textual critics, seek out critics that discuss the topic or the genre or the artistic movement or the cultural context. In fact, **cross-disciplinary comparisons can open up fascinating discussion**. Cultural theory and philosophy, for example, have rejuvenated literary criticism. If you find a critic talking about developments in modernist music forms and it somehow makes sense in the context of Ezra Pound's rejection of mechanical metre use it. What could show intellectual versatility and daring more than the ability to transplant new concepts from surprising sources onto familiar literary material?

Re-presentations

Such intellectual opportunism we recommend highly. As long as you can make it relevant and it enhances your discussion then take the chance. This type of approach is also very useful when looking at how a literary text has been stretched into new forms. Every re-presentation of a literary text will have some guiding principle behind it. So, for example, what is Danny Boyle, a renowned film director, doing to *Frankenstein* by turning it into a play where the actors alternate the roles of Frankenstein and the creature? We could safely assume that he is commenting on the gothic **doppelganger** theme evident in the text, but what else does he prioritise and what does he push to the background? Boyle talks about this and so he can be utilised as a stimulating critical voice; as can the actors Benedict Cumberbatch and Jonny Lee Miller.

If we study Aubrey Beardsley's Victorian illustrations of *The Rape of the Lock*, what do they reveal about the central concerns of the text? When Julie Walters becomes Alisoun, Chaucer's Wife of Bath, how has the original Middle English text been reworked? By making it contemporaneous how is Chaucer's medieval poem still made relevant over 600 years after it was written? In fact, how can a hip-hop retelling of *The Canterbury Tales* work and what does it reveal about the text? (It exists, believe us, we've heard it!)

197

When we hear T.S. Eliot reading his own *The Waste Land* what does this do to the text? How does it alter our response as readers? **Engaging with literary texts in new forms can be a refreshing experience, forcing us to re-examine the original text anew and jolting us out of complacency**.

In the same way it must be argued that you as students should grapple with the same questions when you creatively respond to a literary text. If you condense Pope's poem into a graphic novel how do you go about it? If *A Clockwork Orange* was to be turned into an orchestral score [something we're sure Anthony Burgess would have loved], what would it sound like and how would this relate to the text? **Creative responses are hugely useful portals into literary texts** and hence any teacher worth their salt will use them. There is a whole host of executive decisions to be made about how to do this. Ultimately, you have to grapple with the realities of using a new form to transmit the same core messages. **What may be lost and what can be gained through such creative transformations can sometimes reveal more about a text than any critic will be able to**. That's the theory anyway. Speaking of which, it's time to unpick the ideas underlying critical approaches and turn what we like to see as our laser-guided attention to the famously tricky subject of literary theory....

19. Using Critical Theory Effectively

How is critical theory different from criticism? This question will define the introduction to any university course on the subject and is too huge an intellectual journey to condense usefully here. However, we will try! To delight our inner postmodernists, this review can never be more than surface depth, really.

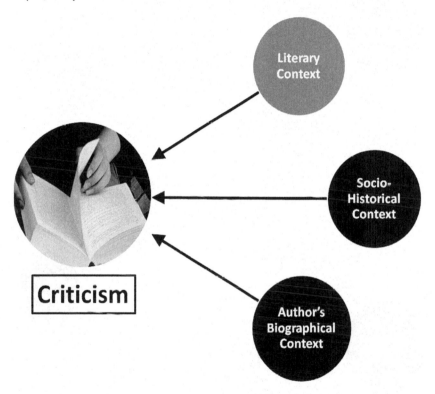

The essential difference between criticism and theory revolves around the literary text itself and how it is viewed. Criticism examines the text; theory takes a step back to examine the ideas and approaches underpinning both the text and its criticism, as well as the fundamental nature of both of these elements. **Criticism is always text specific and bestows primacy on the text above all else, whereas theory is more interested in how culture operates; and consequently, how texts operate in culture**. Therefore, the focus shifts from the text to the culture. In this regard, critical theory is similar to context, which shows how meaning is generated in literary texts by culturally specific events. One helpful way of explaining the difference between the two is that **critical theory seeks to show what the text reveals about cultural values, whereas context seeks to show how the cultural events are reflected by the text.**

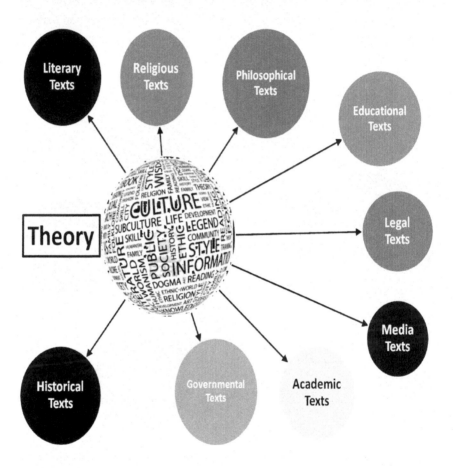

Theory can become very complicated very quickly, as is apparent here. It is an intellectual subject with formidable levels of difficulty and we view it as a useful tool in engaging with literature, but no more than that. Our approach is always to prioritise the text over the theory. What follows is a brief outline of the basic principles guiding each of the major theoretical approaches and some examples of how they can be implemented successfully at A-Level. For an excellent introduction into the murky waters of critical theory, we would recommend Peter Barry's *Beginning Theory: an Introduction to Literary and Cultural Theory.*

The Development of Theory

Critical theory is a relatively recent phenomenon and evolved as a response to what is known as **liberal humanism**. Liberal humanist critics saw the meaning of a text as contained essentially within the text itself. Contextual factors were useful but not essential to establishing such meaning; instead close textual analysis disconnected from socio-historical factors revealed true meaning. Liberal humanists also tended to equate literature with moral instruction; the greater the literature the more morally useful it was.

How readers accessed this moral message was to trust the critic, who would mediate between text and reader to reveal this. This approach then sees **literature as the container of universal truth about human existence; great literature becomes a timeless thing transcending cultural change**, an attitude that could also be applied to human nature itself. As we have shown before, the hierarchy was clear: visionary critics worked out what the God-like genius author had to say and spread the word to the lay people, aka the humble reader.

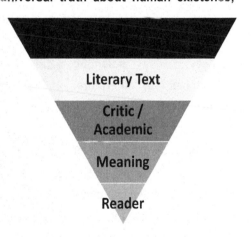

Literary Text

Critic / Academic

Meaning

Reader

It would not take a genius to speculate that such an approach to literature would be inherently limited. **After a number of critics have interpreted the text there can be nowhere else to go.** Such a literary cul de sac was reached in the 1960s. The time was ripe for a radical new approach. The combination of social anxieties arising from World War two and the subsequent Cold War, the realisation of instability and uncertainty lamented as far back as the Modernists coupled with the countercultural revolution of the 1960s itself produced new approaches to literary study. **In short, the study of literature became political.**

The universal nature of liberal humanism's messages was challenged and this ignited a radical new reformulation of the literary text. Now, the literary text was seen as a cultural product; impossible to separate from the cultural values that informed it. The liberal humanist hierarchy previously mentioned was usurped as the concept of reader-response and the notion that the author is dead [thank you, Roland Barthes] revolutionised literary criticism. Concepts like truth, human nature and literary meaning became unstable, ever-changing, culturally constructed and ultimately, never completely knowable.

Obviously, such a radical new vision of society and literature necessitated new methods on interpretation. Whereas the liberal humanists tended to have very personal critical voices, **the new critics used theoretical principles drawn from social studies, linguistics and neuroscience to create more objective, almost scientific approaches to literature.** Marxist theory and Freud's theory of psychoanalysis were well established but had never been applied in literary setting before. **A new explosive plurality of meaning was**  **born for literature study; a plurality that is still evolving to this day**.

So let's get acquainted with these new theoretical approaches. We have decided that rather than build a chronological sequence that shows the how the various critical schools developed and fed into one another, it will be much more productive to consider the theoretical approaches most helpful for A-Level literature study. We'll then illustrate how the theories can be applied to a literary texts using Sheridan's Georgian play, *The Rivals,* as this is a play on which there is relatively little critical commentary. This stuff isn't easy, so take a deep breath, and bear with us. Feel free to skip between the explanation of a theory and its practical application with regard to *The Rivals*.

Marxist theory

Marxist critics are most concerned with establishing the mechanisms of **social power** in a text and literature can be seen merely as a dramatisation of such power struggles. Ultimately, the text is nothing more than a social product, much like a chair or elaborate rug, and it is inevitable that this social product will reflect the values of that society. They seek to identify evidence of a **hierarchical class system** and how these different classes interact in the text. Class conflict is all about social power and economic advantage and Marxist critics examine a text to find out how social power is maintained by those in power.

Consequently, evidence of **repressive state structures** [police, soldiers, law courts etc] and **ideological state structures** [religion, education, art etc] are of great interest to Marxist critics. The social background of the author will also be significant to Marxists, as they seek to investigate the connection between this and the messages transmitted in the text.

Key Concepts: economic power of ruling elite; oppression of working classes; control systems of the rich; relationship between art and economic power; interpellation - the idea that the individual is constructed as a consumer by capitalist ideologies

Key Theorists: Karl Marx, Louis Althusser, Terry Eagleton

Psychoanalytical theory

Sigmund Freud's theory of the mind is the key to this approach. Based upon the belief that all human behaviour is driven by **primal desires that must be repressed** or controlled by our conscious, or ego, this approach focuses on what is hidden in texts. This conflict of repressed desires leads to a surface-depth analogy, where surface behaviour must be

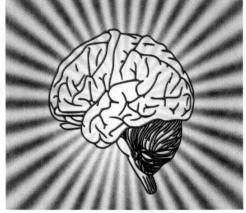

analysed to reveal the motivations hidden deep in the unconconscious, or id. Psychoanalytical theorists, therefore, focus specifically on locating hidden or repressed desires in texts and pinpointing the conflict between outward behaviour and the unspecified outcome of such behaviour.

Freud maintained that the unconscious cannot be accessed except through **dreams** and he developed a system of dream analysis revolving around **symbolism and implied meaning**. For Freud, Literature expressed the unconscious dreams and fears of society. Consequently, psychoanalysts are particularly interested in symbolism and how this operates in texts. Most controversial of all Freud's concepts is that of the **Oedipus complex**, where the male child desires to kill the father figure and realise sexual desire with the mother figure; desires that are repressed in all males according to Freud. This theory is often used to discuss intergenerational power struggles in literary texts.

Key Concepts: repressed desires and how they drive behaviour; conflict between the id and the ego; dreams as articulation of id

Key Theorists: Sigmund Freud, Jacques Lacan

Feminist theory

Feminist critics argue that our notions of **masculinity and femininity are social constructs** rather than innate qualities; in other words, we are born male and female but we must learn to behave like men and women. Given the patriarchal dominance of most societies in history, portrayals of female experience have been/is controlled and validated by men, not women. Laura Mulvey, a feminist film critic, calls this presentation of the world from a dominantly male perspective '**the male gaze**.'

Consequently, feminist critics are concerned with the presentation of femininity and the relationships of power between men and women in literary texts. They seek to expose the **patriarchal mechanisms** that portray the female as an exotic 'other', a being defined by not being male, an object to be aesthetically admired as opposed to a complex subject in her own right.

Key Concepts: limited male presentations of women; systems of patriarchal power; articulation of authentic female subjectivity

Key Theorists: Elaine Showalter, Julia Kristeva, Catherine Belsey

Postcolonial theory

Postcolonial theorists take the concerns of Marxist and feminist critics and reconfigure them through the prisms of **race or ethnicity**. Colonialism exists as part of the exploitative processes of European capitalism and such colonising powers felt free to construct the colonised peoples they exploited as, similarly to women, **exotically 'other.'** The same limited and reductive stereotypes are perpetuated through social discourse; the type of discourse that designates the coloniser as civilised and rational and the colonised as uncivilised, irrational, lazy etc. **The colonised becomes the anti-coloniser**.

Postcolonial theorists search literary texts for such representations of foreignness or to reveal the prejudiced values that promote such representations. Postcolonial critics also look for examples of **cultural hybridity**, where notions of oppositional ethnic identities are broken down by mixing i.e. one way to destroy power structures based on white and black skin colour is to mix them so the original dialectical relationship is destabilised.

Key Concepts: skin colour or ethnic identity as primary means of subjectivity; socially constructed concept of white as normal; oppositional binaries of white and other ethnic minorities; limiting presentation or ethnic identities

Key Theorists: Frantz Fanon, Edward Said, Homi Bhabha

Structuralist theory

Structuralists believe that language creates the world we live in not the other way round and hence reality must adhere to the types of structural patterns found in language. They see the **world as a set of interconnected structures**, where meaning is generated in relation to these other structures and this extends to

the literary text. Consequently, they search for **patterns** within the text as well as looking at patterns outside the text.

Structuralists view the text as part of **wider, containing structures** such as the history and conventions of genre, intertextual formations, even the function of specific art forms. It is immediately obvious that structuralist critics quickly move away from the text to the wider realms of literature, history and social discourse, leaving close textual analysis of the text behind. Even when engaged at a textual level they are not concerned with the content as a means to establishing meaning. Rather they look at how structural patterns in content create meanings.

Again, they look to find patterns of all types [echoes/reflections/parallels/ contrasts/distortions] at different levels in the text [plot/ character/language/setting/structure]. More often than not these patterns organise themselves into **oppositional pairings or binaries** across the structural layers to produce an overall structural coherence i.e. light/dark, animal/human, first person narration/omniscient narration, order/chaos etc.

Key Concepts: all texts are interdependent and exist in series of different structures; texts display oppositional pairings on various structural levels; meaning in language is relational (we understand words not through their connection to physical reality, but through their relationships to other words in the linguistic system).

Key Theorists: Claude Levi-Strauss, Roland Barthes

Poststructuralist theory

Poststructuralists are related to structuralists in a way that time does not permit us to explain fully here. Poststructuralists are the angst-ridden and troublesome adolescent siblings of structuralists. In fact, the key structuralist, Roland Barthes, makes a transition to poststructuralism in his later work, especially in his essay "Death of an Author," which, as you know, denied authors absolute power over a text's meaning and bestowed power on the lowly reader instead. Both structuralism and poststructuralism start with the concept of language as creating the world. Ultimately, structuralists see the structural patterns associated with texts as signs of their stability and coherence. By contrast, poststructuralists are much more radical and pessimistic, focusing instead on the random, arbitrary nature of language. They assume that language is fundamentally unreliable and, hence, so is any attempt at stable meaning or certainty of communication.

Instead of locating structural patterns, **poststructuralists are more interested in contradictions, paradoxes, omissions, gaps**. Textual disunity rather than unity is the post-structuralist order of the day. This textual disorder is extended to the wider world in general, creating what is known as a **decentred universe**; one where all sources of previous certainty and reliability have been destroyed. What does this practically mean in terms of examining literary texts? It means that the poststructuralist seeks to reveal **contradictory meanings** in a text teasing out what they call 'warring forces of signification'; if a text seems to say one thing the poststructuralist will seek to uncover meanings that contradict this! You will notice that meaning here is always plural, never singular. One single meaning is impossible for poststructuralists as meaning becomes self-contradictory and constantly in flux.

Key Concepts: the impossibility of stable meanings; texts as inherently contradictory and fragmented; meaning not generated by author but by readers

Key Theorists: Roland Barthes, Jacques Derrida

Postmodern theory

Postmodern theory takes the decentred universe identified by post-structuralists and celebrates it. Postmodernists revel in the uncertainty of the modern world and the slipperiness of meaning that this entails. Postmodernism is also a **response to how Western culture has become**

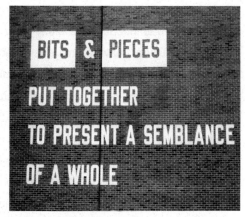

dominated by visual images and how this has contributed to what is termed the 'disappearance of the real', where the reproduced image rather than the original object is most important.

They reject modernist laments of about lack of certainty and promote a playful approach to literature. Postmodernists revel in the **mixing of genre conventions, in self-reflexivity, irony, parody and pastiche**. Postmodernists also examine texts to find hybrid blends of high and low culture. If **old forms can be recycled and used in new and exciting ways** then postmodernists will celebrate this. Not only has the universe become decentred, but the self has become decentred - we are constantly aware of our inner contradictions rather than our unities and there is a part of us that is always unknowable. Postmodernists see this as liberating rather than constraining - we are all on an exciting journey of never-ending self-discovery! These elements, along with a consideration of the hypervisuality of the modern world, will excite a postmodernists critic in a literary text.

Key Concepts: celebration of contradiction; embracing of popular/low culture; cultural recycling - using old forms/conventions in new unusual ways

Key Theorists: Jacques Lyotard, Jacques Baudrillard

Okay, you can breathe out now. This gallop through the main theoretical schools may suffer due to its brevity, but we hope it gives enough of a flavour for you to want to investigate them more thoroughly. As the title suggests, this book's main focus in about how to write literature essays. Hence, we have neglected to introduce the many other theoretical schools; such as new historicism, cultural materialism, queer, ecocriticism etc. For more info, please talk to Professor Peter Barry. The summaries are intended to give you an idea of what these various approaches prioritise and suggest some guiding principles that can then be applied to the texts you study.

We recommend that you are at least aware of the major theoretical approaches at AS and can refer to them broadly where necessary. At A2, you will need to become more conversant in the various theoretical schools and their particular concerns and how they can be used to throw additional light on the texts you study. Critical theory will play a fundamental role in any study of English literature at university level, so getting to grips with it earlier rather than later will really stand you in really good stead. The more you engage with theory, the less intimidating and more rewarding it becomes.

Why bother?
(Or what literary theory can do for you that nothing else can)
So how do we put these various theoretical schools into practice and, more fundamentally, why bother? One of the main advantages of applying theory to a literary text is that it can reveal hitherto unexplored paths to interpretation. Another advantage can be to open up obscure texts or texts with very little critical response. To this end, we will now briefly apply some of these theories deftly to Richard Brinsley Sheridan's *The Rivals*, a text neglected by serious critical theorists for several good reasons, none of which we intend to explore here. However, it is a productive process.

Sheridan's play is a pretty limited comedy of manners from 1775 and certainly limited in its theoretical potential. However, what does the application of theory reveal? It must be stressed that the application of theory here is very light touch and in no way comprehensive - it acts more to illustrate how different aspects of the play come into focus with the application of each different critical lens.

If we take a **Marxist** stance we find firstly a play about the leisured classes for an upper-middle class audience. The play presents a ruling elite and an inferior serving class. The fact that Sheridan makes these servants (David and Lucy) smarter or more moral than the people they serve is an in-joke. **In a society revolving around social place, the idea that the lower classes were more intelligent or more moral than their masters was laughable.** See the social construction of social roles there? Also a Marxist will identify the way the servants begin to ape their masters, particularly Fag's smug superiority over his fellow servants. However, any Marxist worth their salt would lament Fag's entrapment in a system that exploits his labours and his inability to see progression as possible to imagine outside the service of his 'betters.'

A Marxist viewpoint might also take a special interest in the marriage market that is dramatised in the play. The transfer of money between families remains firmly within the ruling elite; hence why Lydia Languish's fantasy of elopement and the subsequent loss of inheritance must be shown as ridiculous by Sheridan. All the potential marriage matches are extremely narrow in their social vision; nowhere is there the suggestion of interclass union. Like so many societies before and after, the Georgians were under no illusion that money was power. And that power had to remain in upper class hands, at all costs.

In fact, Sheridan himself was more aware of this than most of his audience. A natural outsider due to his Irishness and his lowly status as son of a theatre manager, he suffered from financial difficulties all his life; mostly self-inflicted, of course. However, he used every method to break into this powerful social group. Ultimately, the writing of *The Rivals* was solely motivated by financial gain. At the time of producing *The Rivals* in 1775, there were only two theatres in London [Drury Lane and Covent Garden] and both under the control of King George III. In fact, Sheridan had to submit his play for royal approval due to the 1737 Licensing Act.

Marxist critics would now begin to move away from the literary texts to identify this clear mechanism of state ideology. Anything deemed threatening to the social power of the ruling elite could be silenced effectively, especially given the mass communication possibilities of the theatre.

<u>Feminist</u> critics would also be interested in such pervasive ideologies in the play but instead focusing on the constructs of gender. **The most obvious focus will rest on the limited role of women in the play**. Lydia Languish, Julia Melville and Mrs. Malaprop are seen as no more than domestic entities. In fact, their imprisonment indoors is very clear in the play. Their servants go outdoors on their behalf and even in the climactic duel scene in Kingsmead

Fields the women must be accompanied by a male. The extremely limited characterisation would certainly rankle with feminist critics [though this could equally be levelled at all of Sheridan's characterisation]. Lydia is portrayed as a petulant child, Julia's worthiness is her endurance of Falkland's neurotic antics while Mrs. Malaprop is famed for her inadequate mastery of language. It's a pretty limiting and depressing range of female subjectivity.

The play also projects a view of women as ultimately irrational, conceited and no more than pretty baubles transferred between men. Sir Anthony's tirade about female education makes it clear that intelligence is not required in women; rather it is merely the basics of domestic management that a woman must possess. Furthermore, Mrs. Malaprop's weak counter argument posits that they need conversational skills also; to cultivate the art of enticing men to be their husbands. A good contemporary work to consult would be Mary Wollstonecraft's *A Vindication of the Rights of Women* which criticises the education of women at that time. Lydia's addiction to sentimental novels shows women to be fantasists, a clear foil to Jack Absolute's financial pragmatism, but also indicates where women found an education of sorts.

Mrs. Malaprop's age is shown to be a clear disadvantage, especially in the cruel final scene where she is passed from suitor to suitor only to be rejected by them all. Her lack of physical beauty has left her no bargaining power in a society where young, beautiful women are desired. Sheridan's second wife, the unfortunately named Esther Ogle, was 19 to Sheridan's 43; which would bring feminist critics to the thorny subject of marriage. Sir Anthony is

Julia's guardian and controls who she marries, so female choice is negated by male values; very much like how Lydia must bow to Jack's desires for her inheritance. **Ultimately, the dowry system that exists at this time equates marriage with financial transaction. This of course transforms young women into financial investments and further objectifies them**. It also promotes the idea that a husband receives a type of financial compensation for taking the burden of a wife.

A **postcolonialist** would have scant pickings, but certainly would be interested in Sir Lucius O'Trigger, the stage Irishman. The existence of such

a character in the theatrical landscape of a colonial power speaks volumes. **The stage Irishman is a limited stereotype, an entire nation trapped within the confines of ultimately a figure of fun**. Sir Lucius is someone to be laughed at, impersonated, an ethnic ventriloquist's doll; defined by his quick anger and aggression he is deemed an inappropriate member of the ruling elite. The irony of stereotypical belligerence in a nation decimated by Oliver Cromwell's colonial violence in the previous century would not be lost on a postcolonialist. Neither would the irony of the outrage at Sheridan's original depiction of O'Trigger. He was criticised for making O'Trigger too vulgar in the first performance; maybe it was too close to the bone for Sheridan's genteel audience. **Postcolonial critics would also be interested in Sheridan's Irishness, a social disability he had to overcome by training himself to look, sound and behave like an English gentleman**; a skill promoted by his father, Thomas, and his academy of elocution, set up in Bath. A postcolonialist would also travel to another of Sheridan's plays *The School for Scandal* where the physical trappings and huge financial rewards of colonialism are made clear. Sir Oliver's huge fortune made in India is controversially presented as the natural spoil for a civilised country.

Psychoanalysts will certainly examine the modes of desire evident in the play. The moral prudery of Georgian England prevented explicit desire from surfacing on the stage, so where is it hidden? One of the places it clearly resides is in the sentimental novels that Lydia Languish devours. While there are no dreams to analyse, the landscape of Lydia's leisure reading is clearly presented as a wish fulfilment, a fantasy that has no realistic hope of existing alongside the financial realism  that really drives marriage in the play. While on one hand such works portray women as irrational and emotionally unstable, they also serve the purpose of arousing excitement. Lady Mary Wortley Montagu described the pioneer of the sentimental novel, Samuel Richardson, like so: "I heartily despise him and eagerly read him, nay, sob over his works in a most scandalous manner". While it may not be proto-"Fifty Shades of Grey" it certainly sounds exciting. Just a quick glimpse of the titles suggests Lydia's sexual awakening and gathering romantic energies: *The Fatal Connection*, *The Delicate Distress*, *The Innocent Adultery*, *Roderick Random*. Even *The Man of Feeling* could undergo Freudian slippage to become *The Feeling of Man*! In general, **what is apparent is that female desires have no place in Georgian society; they are dangerous to social stability and pave the way for the Victorian construction of sexless, pure females in the next century**. Lydia's romantic fantasies must give way to the proper conduct of a wife.

But what of male desires? **It is very clear that male desire revolves around money and status, none of which is repressed in any way, which would make a Marxist weep**. The most interesting, repressed male desire

seems to spring from duelling. Freud's argument that men are attracted to pleasure had to be modified after World War I to include its opposite, desire for destruction. The most obvious example of this reckless abandonment is Sir Lucius O' Trigger's unquenchable desire for danger and violence. As the foil to Bob Acres' comic cowardice he is a strange character, operating outside the bounds of common sense: "three or four feet between the mouths of your pistols is as good as a mile." In fact, **the entire duelling tradition as a spectacle of male bravado would interest psychoanalysts, where the phallic nature and penetrative capabilities of the swords coupled with the muskets' orgasmic explosions of violence could be construed as**

manifestations of repressed homoeroticism. Certainly, they would investigate the intergenerational conflict in the play, where the tension between Jack and Sir Anthony, could be explained as Oedipal in some way. However, the lack of a mother figure has necessitated a substitute: Lydia. Certainly, Sir Anthony's over-enthusiasm about worshipping Lydia's youthful beauty could be seen as the rivalry typical of Oedipal conflict.

The **structuralist** would be interested in the various oppositional patterns in the play, which could be listed like so:

- youth/age
- male/female
- city/country
- bravery/cowardice
- truth/deception
- insider/outsider
- order/chaos
- **clarity/confusion**
- refinement/vulgarity
- romance/marriage
- theatre/novel
- biography/fiction
- audience/playwright
- upper class/working class
- coloniser/colonised
- Restoration comedy/Sentimental comedy

All of these pairings could be used to ground the text itself in a matrix of various connections that would allow interesting discussion. We have marked one particular pairing in bold because this would be picked up on immediately by a post-structuralist.

Post-structuralists would examine how the confusion/clarity pairing relates to both the assumed identities, which generates so much plot confusion in the play, but also the confusion of expression which is most closely associated with **Mrs. Malaprop. Her famous malapropisms unintentionally create new meanings from those that are intended; she is a dramatisation of the unreliability of language**. Interestingly, Sheridan constructs her malapropisms so that they explicitly connect to linguistic terminology. Malaprop's desperation to master language only reveals how language masters her and how the play of multiple meanings allows her intended sentiments to be endlessly distorted and thwarted by language itself. A post-structuralist would also connect this to Sheridan's other major play *The School for Scandal*, where the character Joseph Surface, represents how language can be used as a mask to hide motivation; how a roguish wolf can be hidden in the fleece of a seemingly good sheep / speech.

A post-structuralist might even attack the play's title. We think it is safe to assume that the meaning of a rival is common knowledge. However, to examine the etymology of the word [its origins] it suggests something crucially different. According to www.dictionary.reference.com it originates from Latin and literally means "one who uses a stream in common with another." This suggests no competitive element whatsoever but rather its opposite: working together cooperatively. This might explain the obsolete usage of the word, which signified "a companion in duty." **From the very off, the play's meaning is slipping. This new unfamiliar meaning of rivalry, which now connotes alliance**, could be seen in the way that aristocratic males must work together as a group to ensure that their elite social status is maintained through the medium of marriage. Moreover, given that the love rivals of the play – Jack Absolute, Bob Acres, Lucius O'Trigger and even Faulkland –

represent different aspects of their author any decent self-respecting post-structuralist would highlight this as an example of **a decentred self**. Sheridan's characters reflect the plurality of his own identity – rather than being one self, he is several selves; he is multiple, fragmented and in conflict with himself. In other words all the rivals Sheridan should worry about are contained within himself.

Theory of the self?

It is a good idea to think about your own approach to texts in a general sense. What theoretical school would you most align yourself with or are you more fluid in your theoretical alliances? What aspects of a text are you naturally drawn to? It might be a good idea to think about this...now! Write them down. It is a useful self-reflective approach, which identifies your natural bias.

Doing this alerts you to your intellectual comfort zone. **If you know you subscribe to one predominant school of thought, we again recommend trying out new critical viewpoints when approaching literary texts**. The enforced change in perspective can be both refreshing and useful. If you are an indignant Marxist most of the time, try your hand at being a post-structuralist for a change; if your feminist rage isn't paying dividends pretend you're a postcolonialist instead. Even if it's just for a short time. You may just be surprised by the new angles you create, which could allow you to formulate new, unexpected possibilities as an intellectual adventurer.

It must be stated that each theoretical approach has its own failings. There is no one dominant school that is more useful or more true than all the others. Literary study would be both much easier and also much less interesting. **As we alluded to previously, there is no one high-priest of truth rather there's a gaggle of preachers all vying for your attention. Give them all a fair hearing. Then make your own mind up**. But don't be afraid to convert to another religion if the message doesn't suit; even if your conversion is short-lived. Each theory will privilege certain aspects of a text, while downplaying or simply ignoring other aspects. The usefulness of a given theoretical approach will depend on how compatible it is with your chosen text and how much new light it sheds. Sometimes you have to throw your theoretical paint at the wall and see what sticks!

You might decide that theory is not for you and that you prefer a more text-based approach. Don't fret; we accept all kinds here and are glad of the diverse company. Play to your strengths but stay open-minded at all times.

20. Using Contexts Effectively

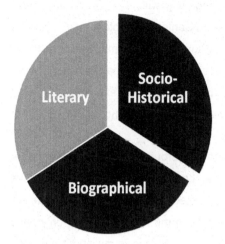

What is context and why do you need to worry about it? Practically, you need to worry about it because you lose AO3 marks for not having it in your essays. On a more intellectual level, **you need to understand that a literary text is not something that exists in a vacuum. It is a cultural product; something written by an author at a certain point in time in a culture that prioritises certain cultural values.** A text can of course be studied independently and this is probably the best starting point for any text as it makes you engage with it at an intense textual level. The more contextual knowledge you accumulate the further away from the text itself you can drift. You must balance this drift carefully. At the end of the day your essay should focus on the literary texts first and foremost, with contextual information adding high polish to your analysis. It should never gleam so much that upon closer inspection there is very little but context to be found. Historians disguised as literature students beware!

Context is that part of the text that places it in a wider framework of different circumstances. Some of these may or may not have any relation to the text itself. For instance, compare Kurt Vonnegut's *Slaughterhouse Five* with Geoffrey Chaucer's *The Canterbury Tales*; two narrative tricksters writing roughly 550 years apart. The major cultural event of Vonnegut's time is World War II while the major cultural event in Chaucer's time is the Black Plague. Both events had catastrophic cultural impacts upon European civilisation, both in terms of population and outlook on life. But, whereas Vonnegut's narrative is an explicit response to the firebombing of Dresden, the Black Plague is nowhere to be found in Chaucer. Instead, it is the cultural effects on medieval England that he records as an implicit response to the plague.

Without this extra-textual knowledge, engaging with *The Canterbury Tales* would be an impoverished experience. Contextual factors add layers of meaning to a text; appreciation and evaluation of the importance of these layers results in the best literature essays. It also makes for the most stimulating intellectual engagement for both student and examiner. So what are the different types of context you will need to understand?

The most obvious context and the most dangerous one in our opinion is the context of the author's life. You must be very careful with an author's **biography**. Firstly, as we have already noted, **the meanings in a text are not direct reflections of an author's intentions**. Secondly, we only have indirect access to an author's life; what we know we know about them we know through other texts, texts that themselves are open to different interpretations.

Only draw upon biography where it is relevant to your essays and also where it is actually useful. Whereas it might be productive to point out that the anxieties about parenting and children in *Frankenstein* might reflect Mary Shelley's turbulent experiences of family life and tragic loss of infant children, it might be pushing it a little to say that Frankenstein creates a creature of his own because Mary Shelley wanted to control textually what she could not in real life. Again, the horror of childbirth as portrayed in the creation scene in *Frankenstein* could well relate to her own traumatic experiences of childbirth as well as her internalised guilt about her mother dying after giving birth to her. Biography should only be used where strong, useful connections can be made.

Socio-historical context can be very productive but can also be quite distracting at times. It can also require substantial research, so be careful about your time demands. Such context essentially captures the cultural moment of production, to be very Marxist about it.

- What was happening at the time the author was writing?
- What were the major cultural events or raging cultural debates or important cultural values at that time and how can they be seen to influence the text?

So to use Shelley again, **the major socio-historical event of her time was the French Revolution of 1789. But where de we find this in her novel?** Look to the trial of Justine and Victor's scathing attack on the justice system of Geneva; maybe even the plight of Safie and the De Lacey's, which sounds like a reference to the reign of terror after the revolution itself or maybe even the French government's aggressive martial presence in Switzerland after 1798. The creature itself has been interpreted symbolically as representing the rise of the bourgeoisie in France with Victor representing the displaced aristocracy. The sustained debate about parental responsibility makes sense in this context where the creature rightly points out Victor's obligations to care for the creature's welfare.

Or, if we consider Shakespeare's plays, we might examine **how these texts reflect the changing nature of the society in which the playwright lived, as what historians call the 'early modern period' emerged painfully from**

the medieval. Sometimes it may be possible to connect a play to a specific historical event that will give it greater resonance. For example, the performance of *King Lear* to King James' court on Saint Stephen's Night 1606. At other times, context forms the intellectual and cultural backdrop for the debates, tensions and stories Shakespeare's characters embody. Hamlet's famous procrastination, for instance, can be read socio-historically as being rooted in his liminal state, caught between medieval, aristocratic notions of revenge and a more reflective modern and humanistic sensibility trying desperately to develop a new conception of justice.

Literary context is an especially important one and it can be the type of context that achieves very high marks. To excel here you must be able to talk

about how your chosen text relates to the wider literary circles it may align itself with, or in some cases literary movements it rejects or sets itself up in opposition against. To remain consistent we need to stay with our friend with benefits, *Frankenstein*. **It is common knowledge that it is a Gothic text as well as a Romantic text. But we would say that it can also be seen as a science-fiction text, or a crime fiction text or a bildungsroman**. To be assured in your argument you will need to know your Ann Radcliffe from your Samuel Taylor Coleridge, your Raymond Chandler from your Sophocles. You must be able to identify the key values of each genre or style or movement and show how they are used by Shelley in her texts. So we must know about Gothic doubling and eerie settings, Romantic sublimes and male imaginative creativity, the Sci-Fi novum, the similarities between the creature and Oedipus. This also extends to the writer's other works. Do you know much about *The Last Man* or *Maurice* or her short stories? How relevant is the father-daughter incestuous tension in *Matilda* to your understanding of *Frankenstein*? If so, how can you relate them to *Frankenstein*? Can you connect the Romantic education found in *Maurice* with that of the creature's? Of course you can! As long as it is relevant to your essay, you will score high AO3 marks.

Our two most important recommendations are not to include a ready-made context paragraph and not to overuse context. It should be used to illuminate your discussion, not pad it out. The only problem with the theory  that it's useful to have a catch-all context paragraph readily applicable to whatever title you're given is that it's entirely wrong. **You will earn precisely no marks for any reference to context that isn't contributing to the development of your argument.** We'll come back to this in the next paragraph. Be careful too not to overuse context; it can be very easy for an essay to become a biography mixed with a literature essay or a history essay with some literature thrown in free of charge. It is also important to recognise that using context can be a risky exercise in speculation. Your speculations must be wholly convincing. Treat context as you would court evidence: it should prove your point beyond all reasonable doubt.

So suppose you are laden down with jewels of infallible contextual speculation; how do you use them? We would advise against the lazy option, which is the essay writing equivalent of illegal dumping: just plonk in all in one place and let the examiner work out the various connections to the literary text. This lumpen fella is known as the 'context paragraph'. Usually, this factpile can be found either at the very start or the very end of an essay, lurking like a context filled iceberg. **The unfortunate problem with this approach is that is a very inefficient and ineffective way of using**

contextual information. You end up putting in lots of context in a non-specific way so you must put lots in to cover all the various bases. AVOID! Context is something that should be sprinkled through an essay, like salt; adding subtle unexpected flavours, rather than delivering a tastebud overloading ball of facts.

Any context you use should be employed where relevant in your essay; it should reinforce discussion as it happens. Do not expect the examiner to retrospectively apply your context for you. When you use it, make the connections clear: how exactly does context form textual meaning? For example consider the following efforts and evaluate the strengths and weakness of each:

1. *Sherman Alexie's* Reservation Blues *was written in 1994 and explores the plight of Spokane Indians on the reservation. It is a novel full of lonely, alienated characters battling low self-esteem, poverty, depression, alcohol or drug addiction or trauma of some sort. Alexie himself is an Indian. When Junior, Victor and Thomas get together to form the band Coyote Springs, their initial success allows the possibility to leave the reservation and leave the dysfunction of their previous lives behind. Predictably, in Alexie's dark tragi-comedy, this success fails to materialise and the characters return to become more alienated and bitter, like Victor, or cannot go on, like Junior, who commits suicide. Only Thomas succeeds, albeit in a very limited way, as he determines to leave the reservation and seek a new way of life.*

2. *Sherman Alexie wrote* Reservation Blues *in 1994. He is an Indian himself and the book explores what is like to be an Indian living on a reservation. It is a novel but a special type of novel called a magical realistic novel, which he likes because he is an Indian. In America, the Indians were not treated well by the white men and Alexie shows the effects of this in the book. His own mum worked as a counsellor on his own reservation so he knew all about how bad life was for Indians who lived on the reservations. This essay will look at how Alexie explores issues of alienation and*

loneliness in his book.

3. In **Reservation Blues,** *many of the characters are dysfunctional and alienated in some way. Their responses to this situation varies and ranges from alcoholism and drug abuse to violent bullying to fantasy to hopeless inertia. Alexie explores this because he is an Indian. In the novel, Junior commits suicide towards the end because he cannot handle his failure to leave the reservation and the failure of Coyote Springs to land a recording contract. Alexie's shockingly pithy description of his death, "Junior squeezed the trigger," reflects how little self-worth Junior has but also alludes to the common occurrence of such pointless deaths on the reservation. The lives of ordinary Indians and their struggle for survival in an America that wants to erase them from history is a common theme of Alexie's writing; such thematic exploration can also be found in his short story collections* **The Toughest Indian in the World** *and* **The Lone-Ranger and Tonto Fistfight in Heaven.**

4. *The majority of Alexie's characters in* **Reservation Blues** *are blighted by dysfunctional relationships and a type of cultural inferiority that leads to self-alienation and profound existential unhappiness. Alexie chooses to explore these problems, based on his own experiences as a Spokane Indian only too aware of how tough reservation life is, through the unusual narrative strategy of magic realism and a unique brand of tragi-comedy. Big Mom, who "for seven generations [...] had received those horses and held them in her arms," is the most obvious manifestation of this magic realism. The magic realism aspects of the novel can be related to Indian culture's history of oral storytelling and the emphasis on epic myth cycles that are central to Indian heritage. This is most acutely realised in the character of Thomas Builds-the Fire, involuntary storyteller and also chief songwriter and singer with the band Coyote Springs. He is very similar to the various narrators in his short story collection,* **The Toughest Indian in the World;** *another work that brings to light the difficulty of Indians trying to survive in modern America. Alexie proposes that the best way to deal with such cultural alienation is to try articulate the pain it causes. The*

227

other alternatives (alcohol abuse, drug addiction, domestic violence, depression and poverty) are well presented in the novel; problems well known to Alexie from his mother's work as a reservation counsellor.

The novel explores this cultural aftermath of white cultural oppression by initiating its narrative in the 1880s at the height of white-Indian conflict; a fact that is represented in the names of white characters bearing the names of famous cavalry generals from that campaign i.e. Wright, Sheridan, Armstrong. It shows how they still constantly hound and harass Indians more than a century after their violent military campaigns. No wonder they still feel disenfranchised over 100 years after being forced off their lands and onto the reservation.

So, how do these context users shape up? **Example 1** is actually a good piece of writing; a little general and not engaged at textual level but insightful. However, it doesn't use context at all; or certainly not in any meaningful way. It draws attention to Alexie's ethnic origins as an Indian himself but fails to explain why this is important or relevant to the question in hand. It is typical of the type of response that omits a crucial connecting statement, in this case one that explains why Alexie being an Indian is important. Please do not assume that the examiner will be able to read your mind. They can only read what's on the page. So make it very clear what your point is and why it is important.

Example 2 is not bad - it is clumsy but knowledgeable in terms of context. Here may lie one of the main lessons of this book: sometimes it is not enough to simply know, you must be able to use what you know effectively. It is clear that the student knows about Alexie's Indian background as well as the tensions between white and Indian culture. However, they do not connect the context to the topic, which we could safely assume is about the alienation and loneliness in the novel. It also makes a ham-fisted attempt to bring in some literary context through allusion to the narrative strategy of magic realism - it is NOT called magical realistic writing!

Example 3 is much better, mostly due to the detailed specifics it supplies. It uses different types of context, biographical, cultural and literary; and uses them well. It correctly identifies that Alexie's personal experience feeds into his thematic explorations, although it does this in perhaps too sweeping a way. It could have stopped to consider how exactly these topics are so well known to him. However, it does ground its discussion firmly in the text and works niftily out into the cultural context of Indian marginalisation. Again, it is rather sweeping and could do with some more discussion. Linking nicely into Alexie's other works, it does, however, provide some very valuable literary context.

Again, not to insult your intelligence too much, it should be clear that **Example 4** is the pick of the bunch; the top context banana. It is excellent, but not perfect. Context is used very impressively in that it enhances the discussion about why the characters in Alexie's novel are so unhappy. It uses Alexie's biographical context very well, as well as grounding the socio-historical context of the Indian wars of the 1880s in the text itself. It then goes on to link the narrative strategy of  magic realism to the cultural context of Indian customs as well as drawing upon knowledge of Alexie's other works. You will see also that the context constantly contributes to the discussion. A slight negative might be that it is too context heavy and prevents the discussion from really engaging with the text intensely. This is true, of course, but it has been cobbled together mainly for the purposes of showing how context should be used effectively. As stated previously, context should be sprinkled throughout your essay rather than heaped on in mounds where the examiner has to dig down to your main point. Be selective but, more importantly, be effective!

PART THE FOURTH

THE EVIDENCE ROOM

PART THE FOURTH: The Evidence Room

21. Good and Bad Essay Titles

Some teachers will give their students a title, others will allow students to devise their own one. There's no golden rule about what constitutes a good essay title for coursework. That, however, doesn't mean we won't offer some words of advice, of course. For example, it is always helpful to choose titles which encourage you to examine both what the texts have to say and the methods the writers use to say it. In other words, go for titles that focus on exploring how writers **present** their themes / characters / characters relationships. If you want to hone in on a particular aspect of the writer's techniques, you may want to use a title such as 'Examine how writer x uses narrative structure / narrative strategies / language / metaphors to present the theme of y'.

Alternatives to 'explore' include 'examine', 'consider' and 'discuss'. As we established earlier, these are better verbs to employ than other commonly used verbs such as 'describe', 'show' or 'outline' because they indicate that the essay is open-ended, explanatory and aware of different possible readings.

More often than not, your coursework essays will be comparative in nature. In addition to the advice we've already outlined earlier in the book, we advise you to use titles that foreground the comparative aspects of the task. For example, a title like 'Discuss how writers x, y and z present theme T' can be rephrased as 'Compare and contrast the presentation of theme T in the works of writers x, y and z'

The most successful essays develop a clear line of argument, an argument that will be tested through some consideration of counter arguments. Hence titles using phrases such as 'evaluate the view that...' or 'to what extent do you agree that...' are helpful because they emphasise this essential dimension of your essay.

Another key aspect of devising a productive title is to make sure your focus is not too broad or conversely too narrow. You may be comparing two, three or more texts, which means you're handling a mountain of material. It's essential that your title helps you to break down this material effectively. A title asking you to explore the presentation of emotions in *Romeo and Juliet*, *King Lear* and *Hamlet* would obviously be too broad, whereas a question focused on the protagonists' use of the word 'you' would be too narrow (probably). A better question would focus on a specific emotion, such as love. Better still would be to focus on a specific form of love, such as erotic, parental or filial love, or on the relationship between opposite emotions, such as love and hate. Generally it is fruitful to examine what you consider to be the central tensions in your texts.

Sometimes the process of drafting an essay can generate new areas of interest, taking the discussion away from your original topic area. Or it can reveal that there is less to say than you'd thought on a particular aspect. Just as it's always useful to rewrite your introduction after you've completed your first draft, it's perfectly sensible too to adapt your title to fit the essay you've actually written. Just make sure you consult with your teacher(s).

Most exam boards provide sample topics and titles for coursework essays on their websites and your teachers can usually submit titles to be ratified by a coursework advisor. A dud title would adversely affect your chances of reaching the top marks, so make sure you don't choose one!

Titles on single texts

1. Open titles, focusing on thematic concerns:
    - Discuss how Sylvia Plath exposes the pressures on, and expectations of, middle class American women in the 1950's in *The Bell Jar*.
    - How does Ian McEwan explore the concepts of guilt and forgiveness in *Atonement*?
    - Explore the ways in which the theme of rebellion against authority is presented in George Orwell's *1984*.
    - Examine the presentation of violence in Seamus Heaney's *North* poems.

2. Titles focusing on one specific aspect of a text:
    - Analyse the setting of Milbank prison in Sarah Waters' *Affinity* in terms of its relationship to the themes, characters and context of the novel.
    - Explore the significance of Anthony Burgess's use of Nadsat in *A Clockwork Orange*.
    - Examine Tennessee Williams' use of stagecraft in *A Streetcar Named Desire*.
    - Discuss the significance of Shelley's choice of narrative structure in *Frankenstein*.

3. Titles focusing on evaluation of a critical comment:
    - 'The priest in Gerard Manley Hopkins killed the poet'. To what extent do you agree?
    - To what extent do you agree that Cormac McCarthy's *The Road* is 'nothing more than a Zombie movie in fine prose'?
    - 'Guilt is the all consuming passion in *The God of Small Things* by Arundhati Roy'. How far do you agree with this critical opinion?
    - 'A rom-com in second world war dress.' Is this a fair assessment of DeBernieres' *Captain Corelli's Mandolin*?

4. <u>Titles applying a literary comment to a text</u>:

- Keats suggested we should never trust a poem that has too obvious a design on its readers. Consider Tony Harrison's poems in the light of this comment.
- 'A great mind is androgynous' (Coleridge). In what ways does Virginia Woolf explore this idea in *To the Lighthouse*?
- 'Villains are always more interesting than heroes or heroines'. To what extent does this comment hold true in Arthur Miller's *The Crucible*?
- 'As a genre, The Gothic is overly reliant on set piece scenes and a set of overfamiliar motifs'. Explore Bram Stoker's *Dracula* in the light of this comment.

Often if a title is poor it is because it is too generalised and vague. Often it can be sharpened up by narrowing the focus and by adding a few key words. For example, the title on Burgess's dystopian novel was originally 'Explore Burgess's language in *A Clockwork Orange*.' Clearly this title is blurrily unfocused; the whole novel is made of language...so that's an awful lot of material to get through. Far better to zoom in on a specific aspect of the novel's language. For instance, this could be his use of dialogue, his rendering of his characters' thought processes or his use of figurative language. However, the most interesting, impactful language in *A Clockwork Orange*, and an aspect that makes Burgess's book distinct, is Nadsat, so it makes sense to focus our critical attention on this. That word 'significance' is also, well, significant. To achieve the higher grades, it is never enough to discuss a particular aspect of text, such as the setting or the language. Considering the significance of the aspect makes you connect it to the text's ideas, or, in other words its themes.

As we have said before, and now will say for a final time, the small words that direct you to consider a writer's technique turn out to be crucial. Single words such as 'how' as well as phrases such as 'the presentation of', 'use of' and 'the ways in which' signal this focus. Consider, for example the subtle, but significant difference between 'Examine Tennessee Williams' stagecraft' and 'Examine his **use** of stagecraft'. Adding that simple monosyllable changes the question; now we have to connect stagecraft to a wider design, exploring the writer's purpose and the dramatic effects of lighting, music, props and the other aspects of stagecraft. Phrases such as 'to what extent' and 'how far' have a similar function in evaluative titles in which you are being asked to argue a case. The spatial metaphors imply there is an end point where the argument cannot stretch, where it breaks down and ceases to be convincing; therefore there must be somewhere beyond that extent, i.e. a counter argument. Rarely will the best answer to this kind of title be 'to the full extent' or 'to the very end'.

22. Sample Work

<u>Example of A-grade close textual analysis</u>

This extract analyses the depiction of adolescent rebellion in the poet Selima Hill's extraordinary *Bunny*. This extract comes for an A2 comparative essay which achieved full marks. Although our focus here is on the quality of the close analysis, notice too how neatly the two texts are linked in the first sentence:

> In **The Cement Garden**, *even the death of their mother does not seem to dissolve this self-obsession, much like Selima Hill's protagonist, who ignores her own emotional isolation "as she pouts/ while posing on the rim of the bath/ in a bra with cups the size of elastic pudding-basins." (Pyjama Case) Hill uses the alliteration of 'p' and 'b' to create a sort of childlike clumsiness, and sibilance ("what she gets is this enormous house", "a silver spoon is the size of a cold lily") to suggest a cold distance, as well as a child's lisp, combining to create imagery of reaching for an unearned maturity. The majority of Bunny is set in an "enormous house" and so Hill's talents for sonic writing intensify the readers' thoughts of an echoing building, accentuating the teenager's isolation and consequent self-focus. Through her pinpointing of small objects, Hill also creates a wonderful contrast between these seemingly insignificant details and the sheer vastness of the house, standing as a metaphor for the capacity of adolescent opportunity and catalysation of their futures. Her prevailing use of couplets as a poetic framework for Bunny also complements this idea of isolation, which allows every teenager the space to experiment safely and develop themselves.*

In this example, the student demonstrates they are acutely aware of the effect of aural imagery. The effect of recurrent sonic patterns, such as the 'p' and 'b' alliteration, are explored adeptly. Particularly impressive is the astute way the student analyses various aspects of the poem; even more impressive is how she also explores how these aspects work in conjunction. For example, different sound patterns are shown to weave together to create subtle impressions of the central character, and, in turn these sonic aspects are then related to Hill's use of setting and metaphor as well as to the structural aspects, such as the use of contrast and the frame of the couplet form.

We feel this essay is so good we couldn't resist quoting a bit more. You don't need to have read *Bunny* to know this is great, original critical writing. We especially like: the focus again on sound and the effect of aural imagery; the comments on repetition as a key device; the responsiveness to comparisons and to patterns of imagery and the astute linking of these features to the poem's form and structure:

In her poem, Home, the sense of alienation and reclusiveness are enhanced, firstly with the depiction of home as an echoing, isolated place. Hill's use of italics on "home" and "the dead" help the reader recreate this echo in their reading, as does the repetition of the words "mouth", "echoes" and "home". Her comparison of "home" to death furthers this imagery of a dead, secluded environment, perhaps making a comment on relations with the family, but also the physical characterization of the house, Selima Hill literally draws a line of symmetry between them, prescribing the first couplet the role of describing the home, and the second couplet as about death. The symmetry and balance of structure makes the parallels between the two seem much clearer. In Bolero, the girl casts aside her aunt's effort in knitting her a bolero "of powder-blue" – not an intense enough shade of blue to be adolescent – and instead yearns for was "a wet suit/ made of skintight lapis lazuli" in which to presumably flaunt a newly-developed body, and also a garment of much more grown-up, intense blue. The "puff of powder-blue" imitates childish word play to contrast with the 'adult' desires in its alliteration, as is the same for "wanted was a wet suit", and the iambic metre skips along childishly too, certainly in antithesis against the maturity-craving teen.

The two essays which follow demonstrate many of the virtues we have been preaching in this book. As you read them, see if you can recognise these virtues.

Essay 1

To what extent do you agree with the view that the chaos in 'King Lear' is caused by the insubordination of women against male authority?

Lear's haunting final lines, "Why should a dog, a horse, a rat, have life/ and thou no breath at all?" address some of the most significant recurring concerns of the play: why is there evil in the world; why do people act in the way they do; what causes the chaos that crescendoes ever greater from the very first scene?

Many feminist critics, Kathleen McLuskie in particular, have claimed that the play presents women as the root cause of all this evil and suffering; specifically women subverting the patriarchal norms of the world of 'King Lear'. There is certainly a good case for this: Lear's misogynistic tirade in Act 4 is especially suggestive of this view, claiming of women "but to the girdle do the Gods inherit/ beneath is all the fiend's". These associations of the female with Satan, stemming from a long misogynistic tradition of religious philosophy drawn from the story of Eden, suggest that women are the embodiment of temptation and sin in the world ; a force which, as McLuskie claims the play evinces, can only be held at bay by the strength of male power, both in the family and in the state.

However, this feminist view ignores entirely the function of the play's subplot, which is exclusively male. If 'King Lear' were intended merely to show how chaos would ensue as a result of women disobeying men then the subplot would be redundant. However, the presence of a parallel story of insubordination and ensuing chaos, a story which depicts male insubordination, strongly signals that the play is concerned not only with the consequences of female rebellion, but with the wider issue of subversion of patriarchal, hierarchical, half-feudal world order. Doubtless, the insubordination of women plays a significant part, but ultimately it is not just female insubordination that causes the suffering and deaths of most of the significant characters.

Yet the role of female rebellion in the chaos must not be underestimated. McLuskie's observation that the "narrative, language and dramatic organisation all define the sisters' resistance to their father in terms of gender, sexuality and position within the family" is very significant. The inversions of power orchestrated by Goneril and Regan are repeatedly characterised by images of monstrosity and bestial savagery. Lear's hope that Regan will "flay (Goneril's) wolvish visage", Albany's reproval of Regan's assertion of autonomy in Act 5 as "most monstrous" and the servant's closing whisper in Act 3, at the pinnacle of the play's brutality that "if (Regan) live long...women will all turn monsters" combine to present the rebellion of women against their male lords as deeply contradictory to laws of nature such as Tillyard suggests were believed to exist in a hierarchal "Great Chain of Being" ordained by God. By denying their subjugated places in this "chain" the women are seen to be denying their very natures and hence becoming monsters and "gilded serpents" so feared by the play's men. This has particular resonance in a play first produced in 1605, only very shortly after the long reign of an unmarried, therefore unfettered, female monarch. It is not unreasonable to assume that anxieties about a "monstrous regimen of women" rising were widely shared across society.

The correlation between growing female power and the death of their intended Lords (Goneril plots to kill Albany; Regan's husband is killed almost at the precise moment she unleashes the depths of her energies and Lear is cast out into the storm immediately that assert their control of the kingdom) only serves to confirm this reading. Certainly it is essential to note that all three of the sisters who threatened patriarchal order must die before the rebuilding of the kingdom can begin.

Yet it is not only the sisters who must die. So too does the Fool, Oswald, Gloucester, Edmund and Lear; all of whom have acted to undermine the world order of the play. It is as if all dissenters (even unintentional ones) must be cleansed for the hierarchy and its order to be restored. The Fool consistently undermines Lear's authority, accusing him to his face of "being old before he was wise"; Oswald denies Lear's rights as a male and a king by recognising his importance only as "my Lady's father"; Gloucester commits adultery and then resolves to pass his estate to the "whoreson" over the legitimate Edgar; Edmund is almost blasphemous in his plea that "God, stand up for bastards" and even Lear debases the embodiment of the patriarchal authority – the single man placed by God as head of his family and of his state – by trying to carve up his divinely appointed role. The actions of all these men are shown to be destructive to the good order of all who exist in it and, eventually to themselves. Even Kent's "unmannerly" challenge to the maddened Lear in the first scene leads ultimately to a (presumed) declaration of suicide.

The enormity of these crimes against the established hierarchy is emphasised by repeated references to bonds and obligations in the play's imagery, perhaps best exemplified in Kent's disparagement of Oswald that he "like rats oft bite the holy cords a-twain" betraying his lord, Lear. Indeed, the same animal imagery is conferred on males that disrupt the social order as on the females: Kent calls Oswald a "dog" and a "rat"; Edgar when Gloucester believes him to be a traitor is as "unnatural" as Goneril and Regan. Ironically Gloucester, whom Regan perceives as traitorous to her is branded a "fox" for his attempt to be loyal to the king. It is as if the very "cords" that hold society together are being ripped apart from the inside by the emergence of a savage, anarchic spirit which, as Terence Hawkes argues, is most fully embodied in Machiavellian Edmund.

So, then, the play re-cages this spirit by crushing its sources and by re-instating the only two true upholders of the patriarchal hegemony, Edgar and Albany. Only with these two men – legitimate, noble and faithful to the established social structure can the chaos end and order be restored. It is not just female insubordination, but bastardy, the challenging of lords by other *men and the weakness and debasing of patriarchal positions by the very men holding them that cause the chaos in 'King Lear'. And only with the destruction of these rogue elements can society be purged.*

Examiner Commentary

What makes this an excellent A-level essay? Well, by now, we hope that having read this book you'll be able to recognise the quality of this work. Using the assessment objectives we should be able to recognise that:

- ✓ AO 1: The writing is clear, fluent and accurately expressed. The introduction is concise, strikingly incisive and conceptual; the conclusion follows from the clear logic of an argument that is also clear, with shifts between the two sides signalled with discourse markers ('However' and 'yet') Some technical vocabulary is employed (e.g. patriarchal hegemony) and the student shows very good knowledge and understanding of the play.

- ✓ AO 2: Textual evidence is drawn from across the play, from main and subplots, from major and minor characters. Cross-referencing allows the student to explore patterns of significant language, such as the imagery of monstrosity, bonds and of animals. Precise exploration of the latter leads the essay into contesting the argument expressed in the essay title.

- ✓ AO 3: The student finds evidence to both support and contest the titular statement. The weighing of the argument is well considered and well informed, utilising a key critic in this debate, McLuskie. The views of the critic are themselves critiqued in a convincing manner. Other readers, such as the critic Hawkes and the literary historian, Tillyard, are brought in to amplify and illuminate the discussion. These form a background to the student's explanation of their own critical view.

✓ AO 4: Socio-historical information is used to inform the discussion, but does not bog it down. The student brings this information into the debate when they need it. References to contemporary attitudes to women and the implications of the Great Chain of Being are neatly marshalled to support the line of argument.

Overall this is an extremely good, though not perfect essay, especially as it was completed in timed exam conditions. As is obvious, in a coursework essay there is more time and space for deeper consideration of the issues at hand, just as a novel is more commodious than a short story.

Essay 2

Our second sample is an AS coursework essay. This time we will not reveal our marking, but we encourage you to mark this essay yourself against the coursework mark scheme and/or using the AOs.

How are gender roles and stereotypes treated in Regeneration and Fiesta: The Sun Also Rises?

Although written 65 years apart, Fiesta: The Sun Also Rises and Regeneration are set with only a decade between them. They conveniently span both the immediate effects and the aftermath of the war, almost in a continuous stretch. This proximity contributes to a number of thematic connections, due to the anxieties and values of their shared society. A major concern of the general population in America and the UK was homosexuality and emasculation, and it was this controlling society that approved of the treatments shown in Regeneration, encouraging rigid moral conduct and heterosexuality. Karin Westman[1] noted that the culture that Barker was writing about was "not only at war with Germany, but also with itself"; these strict ideologies caused a lot of tension, especially amongst the soldiers in World War 1.

Paul Fussell [2] explains that, despite Honour and Glory being widely recognised and inspiring values associated with the War, the environment that the soldiers were working in was incredibly emasculating. Many of the soldiers volunteered to fight on the grounds that they were fighting for their country and serving a duty to protect the women and children there. This 'promised masculinity' was but a false illusion and as Hemingway said, "abstract words such as glory, honour, courage or hallow were obscene beside [...] the numbers of regiments and dates."[3] Society had very secure ideas of what was wrong and right, which in turn created a mould for citizens to conform into - Sassoon compares this process to a "sausage-machine" in Chapter 23. As shown in the recruiting poster of a father being asked by his children what he did in the "Great War" [4], there were great pressures placed on men to fight and to be chivalrous. In Regeneration, Anderson "still wants to serve his country" (p244) despite his previous trauma from the war and Sassoon, regardless of his protest against it, still feels a duty to return to the Front. Rivers reiterates this when he says "It's his duty to go back, and it's my duty to see he does" (p 73).

Fiesta, on the other hand, shows a number of war veterans who have already experienced the war and realised the insignificance of these abstract terms and so do not pursue them anymore. Two such naïve men are Robert Cohn and Pedro Romero who still appreciate 'Honour' and 'Fair-Play' amidst the background of immorality and dishonesty around them, despite conflict arising around them. Cohn "wanted to make an honest woman" of Brett (p 174) and Pedro's "nice manners" are brought to our attention (p 152); they both want to feminize Brett and make her meet their standards of femininity. It is these characters who seem more effeminate than others, especially the way in which Cohn opens up to his male friends and Pedro is described in a womanly way: his shining black hair, his beautiful style of bullfighting and his tight green pants. In addition, Romero lets Brett dominate him, just as Robert Cohn lets Frances do. Jake hints that Cohn gained the little masculinity he *has as an attempt to prosper and survive in the judgemental, anti-Semitic society he lived in: "He cared nothing for boxing, in fact he disliked it, but he learned it painfully [...] to counteract the feeling of inferiority" (p 1). The men who are openly religious in the book – mainly Cohn and the Christian Romero– seemingly have stronger moral groundings which allude to their femininity. Brett, being an overtly masculine character and certainly not religious, seems to take a liking to these feminine men as though the gender roles in relationships have been reversed. Brett has had affairs with Cohn and Romero whilst undoubtedly enjoying the company of the young, homosexual men at the dance-club too, and at the same time, Jake's romantic inclinations, impotence and emotional sensitivity draw her in. Conforming to gender expectations seems unappealing to Brett and this results in her domineering masculine demeanour that, in return, attracts the feminine men surrounding her.*

The tenderness, gallantry and other feminine emotions represented by certain characters in Regeneration is said to be "so despised [by the soldiers] that they could be admitted into consciousness only at the cost of redefining what it meant to be a man." (p 48) Rivers' treatment encourages talking about these suppressed emotions but he remains aware that the soldiers are resilient against accepting them, due to the emotions feminine connotations. The irony lies in the fact that in order to regain the masculinity they yearn for to return to the Front, they must submit themselves to Rivers' emasculating treatment. John Brannigan [5] observes that during the War, "the social space that women occup[ied] generally expanded, while the space that the men occup[ied] contracted into the trenches." Trench warfare is said not only to have trapped men into these claustrophobic surroundings and emphasized the extent to which they were forced into a type of masculine mould, but that it stretched these social constraints to their extremes too. Meanwhile, the maternal role of officers who had to constantly check on their soldiers' welfare and to look out for them was combined with intimate, comradely relationships, to result in a strengthening of the aforementioned emasculation. Karin Westman herself notes that "the source of men's war neurosis, according to Rivers, is [...] society's compulsory masculinity coming into conflict with the logistics of trench warfare" but that this type of male bonding was crucial in the soldiers' survival, even if it meant going against social norms.

Trauma can be seen as an injury of war, similar to Jake Barnes' impotence. Both the mental and physical injuries presented create despair within the afflicted characters; Jake narrates that "I lay awake thinking and my mind jumping around [...] Then all of a sudden I started to cry." Clearly this 'handicap' prevents him from a sexual relationship with Brett and acts as a castration of his masculinity: "[Jake's] interest in boxing, [...] and bullfighting [...] are not diminished by his impotence, but it compromises his relationships with women" (James Nagel) [6].*The connections between fear, violence and sex can be seen in both books. Fiesta sees Jake's constrained sexual desires mix with the other men's to cause misery and violence. After recalling the violent disputes between Mike, Jake, Robert and Romero, Nagel summarises that "Jake, Mike, Robert, and Pedro have all been injured by Brett's desire..." Romero may seem innocent, but even he vents his rage through bullfighting. Regeneration too sees sexual feelings emerge, even in the midst of the grim and depressing trenches (Prior describes the feeling of going into an attack as "sexy").In some respects, sex is both the cause and the result of violence and this violence is used to try to regain lost masculinity. Prior's courtship of Sarah Lumb draws attention to 'feminine' feelings of tenderness, yet is tinged by underlying violence and hatred. He "both envied and despised her, and was quite coldly determined to get her [...] she should pay" (p 128), his jealousy of her masculinity creating aggressive feelings that he feels he needs to vent.*

To counter this heavy emasculation in the trenches, the men use the violence and thrill of warfare a type of replacement for their damaged masculinity and also to hide their inability to control their feminine tendencies. The bullfighting in Fiesta and the combat in Regeneration both foster masculine feelings of heroism and patriotism whilst releasing a thrill of adrenalin which are seemingly the only way to vent the extreme feelings the men feel, falsely creating a sense of war being the most masculine experience one could have. Jake says himself that "[n]obody ever lives their life all the way up except bullfighters", showing the extent of these feelings that it arouses and in the same way, Prior describes walking into machine gun fire as "sexy" and exciting. John Brannigan writes that "it has become almost taboo to discuss the physical attractions of war for young men in ways that foreground [...]the passion of battle" and that Barker "expos[es] war as an aphrodisiac." Therefore, whilst attempting to regain their masculinity, the soldiers become ashamed of their feelings, which were associated with promiscuity and homosexuality.

The fear of homosexuality was especially prevalent across this era. When Jake Barnes controversially introduces a prostitute to his friends as his wife "Georgette LeBlanc", the famous singer with homosexual tendencies, it causes quite a stir. Likewise when Bill tells Jake that he's fond of him but hurriedly denies that he is "a faggot", there is an air of anxiety about the topic. Jake seems to take an angry stance against homosexuals, perhaps because they have a sexual ability that has been taken from him and yet they don't use it. This opinion is revealed to some extent at the dancing-club where Jake meets Brett; he comments ironically that he thought the people she was with were "a fine crowd" but later unveils his true feelings: "I was very angry. Somehow they always made me angry."Westman points out that at this time "any tendencies towards homosexual love were condemned and often connected to other anti-social behaviour". Certain revulsions against effeminate feelings and homosexuality are clear in Regeneration too: Graves becomes distressed when homosexual soliciting is brought up in conversation and quickly declares his feelings for a girl called Nancy (p 199); Rivers insinuates that homosexuality should be hidden from the public eye by using the case of Oscar Wilde and Robert Ross as a universal metaphor: "I suppose he's learnt to keep his head below the parapet" (p 54).

Sexual promiscuity is a subject that highlights the straight-talking Brett's masculine traits. As shown by her conquest of Romero, she evidently controls her relationships, which was unheard of before the age of the 'New Woman'. Having been already married twice by the age of 34 and with a history of many courtships, Brett hardly seems the discerning, modest type of woman that fitted stereotypes before the war. Nagel takes note of how "Brett's *comments are focused on sexual attraction, speculating about how [Pedro] gets into such tight clothes, stressing his good looks." which was not the expected behaviour for an engaged young woman of the time. Brett's manliness is further described in her physical appearance and her consistent references to herself as a 'chap': "her hair was brushed back like a boy's [...] she was built with curves like the hull of a racing yacht." (p 19)The similarly masculine Sarah Lumb shows her independence from men too with her job at the munitions factory. Her dominant attitude in conversation and course use of language helps to strengthen her character. She is also described as "tall for a woman", with a "cool stare" and the "rate she knocked [drinks] back" (p 89) alarms Prior.*

Frances Cohn could be said to be one of the most masculine woman in both books. She completely dominates her husband, Robert, and started to do so from early on in their relationship with her "absolute determination that he should marry her." (p 5) She is described in a very un-womanly way throughout, most noticeably with her forceful attitude. Hemingway writes that Cohn's "horizon had been absolutely limited to his wife [...]I am sure he had never been in love in his life." (p 7) Compared to previous expectations of women who were supposed to obey their husbands at all costs and to comply with their authority, Frances and other women like her would have been seen as controversial. Even the senior Ada Lumb encourages her daughter to be more critical of herself and meek in her attitude towards men ("you're never gunna get engaged till you learn to keep your knees together." p 194)As well as changing attitudes, "trapped by their ability to reproduce" (Sharon Monteith [7]), women's roles in society were changing too. The 'Munitionettes' in Regeneration show how women kept England running whilst the men were "mobilized into holes in the ground" (Monteith).Irony lies in the fact that whilst they could not reproduce children by reason of their husbands' absence, the reproduction is replaced by the manufacture of weapons and ammunition that was crucial to their men in the trenches. Munitionettes suffered injuries from these dangerous loads (and Betty's attempt at an abortion must be noted too (p 202)), much the same as men did in the trenches; nonetheless men still earned the most money.

Patriarchal relationships were a fundamental part of society before the war. Men were consistently in command over women and they always held the upper hand in family situations. Regeneration and Fiesta both present examples of inverted gender roles within family-type circumstances, the most prominent of these being Rivers' role as a male mother. His attentive position at Craiglockhart exposes his compassionate affections for his patients and it is through his more nurturing type of treatment he practises that the soldiers are capable of their restoration. Whether this devotion rescues them from or submits them to more emasculation is unclear. One thing is for sure though, and that is that Rivers dislikes this effeminate term of "male mother" but cannot escape it. Neurologists like Yealland prefer less gentle treatments like the electric shock treatment and refer to their hysteria in more scientific terms to obscure any femininity by shrouding it with tough, 'masculine' terms. John Brannigan points out that regardless of this, "'hysteria' derives etymologically from the Greek word for womb, it inhibits men for whom masculine endeavour and agency are the key to recovery, and for whom patriotic responsibility is synonymous with heroism" so it truly is impossible to revert the gender subversion.

The two novelists both had personal connections to World War 1; Hemingway was an ambulance driver in Italy, being awarded the 'Italian Silver Medal for Valor' for a self-sacrificing act just weeks after his arrival and Barker's step-grandfather experienced the war first-hand. One might question why Barker and Hemingway should then seemingly criticise soldiers or the war itself, as both of their links to them were through male bravery and heroism, the very concepts that are denied basis or truth in their works. It is true that Pat Barker is widely known to have strong feminist views that may have played a part in this negative attitude but Hemingway's views of women were slightly less certain: David Ferrero [8] says ambiguously that Hemingway "recognized the complexity of masculinity and femininity as well as the dependant relationship between those concepts". Whatever their real views on these matters, it is clear that both authors are keen to communicate the destabilising effects that World War 1 had on previously 'solid 'expectations of gender stereotypes and norms within society.

Bibliography

Texts used:

§ Regeneration (Penguin Books, 1992)

§ Fiesta: The Sun Also Rises (Arrow Books, 2004)

1. Karin Westman,Pat Barker's Regeneration: A Reader's Guide(New York, Continuum, 2001)

2. Paul Fussell, The Great War and Modern Memory (Oxford Paperbacks; New Ed Edition, 2000)

3. Ernest Hemingway, A Farewell to Arms (first published 1929, Scribner)

4. Poster (IWM Q 33122, National Archives, undated)

5. John Brannigan, Pat Barker (Contemporary British Novelists) (Manchester University Press, 2005)

6. James Nagel, Brett and the Other Women in The Sun Also Rises(Donaldson, Scott (ed.), 1996

7. Sharon Monteith, Pat Barker (Northcote House, 2002)

8. David Ferrero,Nikki Adams and the limits of gender criticism (1998)

23. Glossary of Terms

Poetry

Alexandrine - Another name for an iambic hexameter (a six beat line)

Alliteration - the repetition of consonants at the start of neighbouring words

Anapest - a three beat metrical foot, patterned unstress, unstress, stress.

Apostrophe - a figure of speech addressing a person, object or ideas

Assonance - vowel rhyme e.g. bat and cackle.

Ballad - a narrative poem with a swing rhythm of alternating four and three beat lines.

Blank Verse - unrhymed lines of iambic pentameter, famously used by Shakespeare in his plays.

Cadence - The rise and falls of sounds in lines of poetry

Caesura - a marked break in the middle of a line, usually signalled by punctuation

Complaint - a type of lyric poem concerned with mourning

Conceit – an extended metaphor

Consonance - rhyme based on the consonants only. For example, bed and bad.

Couplet - a two line stanza

Dactyl - a three beat metrical foot following the opposite pattern to an anapest: stress, unstress, unstress

Dissonance - a sonic effect that creates clashing sounds

Dramatic Monologue - a poem written in the voice of a character

Elegy - a poem in mourning for a dead person

Elision - the omission of syllables in a word, as in 'oe'r for over'

End-rhyme – rhyming words at end of poetic lines

Enjambment - the running of sentences over the ends of lines and stanzas

Epic - a long poem describing a heroic narrative

Feminine Rhyme - a rhyme that ends with an unstressed or a number of unstressed syllables

Free Verse - non-metrical poetry that does not follow a pre-set form or rhyme pattern

Heroic Couplets - pairs of rhymed iambic pentameters.

Iambic - a two beat metric foot, falling unstress, stress

Iambic Pentameter - five feet of iambs.

Lyric - an emotional, personal poem, often expressing the feelings of the first person speaker

Masculine Rhyme - a line of verse ending on a stressed rhyme

Metre - a regular pattern organising sound and rhythm. Trimeter = a three beat line; tetrameter = four beats; pentameter = five beats; hexameter = six beats.

Octave or Octet - the first eight lines of a sonnet

Ode - a lofty, serious and reflective form of lyric poem

Quatrain - a four line stanza

Refrain - a repeated line or lines at the end of each stanza, like a chorus in a song

Sestet - a six line stanza

Sonnet - a fourteen line poem of which there are three dominant variations, the Petrarchan, the Shakespearian and the Spenserian.

Spondee - two stresses in a row in a line of verse

Tercet - a three line stanza

Trochee, trochaic - a metrical foot with the inverse pattern to an iamb; stress, unstress. For example, William Blake's line *Tyger, tyger, burning bright* is trochaic

Volta - the turning point in a sonnet, conventionally between the octave and sestet.

Prose

Analepsis - another term for a flashback

Bildungsroman - a novel about a character growing up

Dirty Realism - a style of fiction featuring terse, hardened characters, action and language.

Epistolary - a novel written in the form of letters

Focalisation - the management of point of view

Frame Narrative - a story that surrounds another and gives it context

Free Indirect Discourse - a narrative device in which the author and character's perspectives merge; the author adopting the point of view and/or language of a character

Intrusive Narrator - a narrator who explicitly enters into the text to comment on characters and/or action

Magic Realism - fiction in which fantastical events are presented in a realistic manner

Narrative Structure - the way in which the chronological story has been rearranged by the author. For example, in *Frankenstein* the same story is told first by Frankenstein and then by his creation, allowing us to compare their versions.

Omniscient Narrator - a narrator who has a God-like perspective on characters and action

Prolepsis - another term for a flashforward

Drama

Anagnorisis - the moment in which the central character (the protagonist) realises a fundamental truth about their situation which they have not understood before.

Aside - words spoken by a character as if to the audience, unheard by the other characters

Catharsis - the emotional release of tension the audience experience at the end of tragedies, according to Aristotle

Comedy of Manners - a play which ridicules the social conventions of a society

Farce - a slapstick type of comedy in which comic situations are pushed to an extreme of improbability

Hamartia - In tragedies, a flaw in the central character that leads to their destruction

Kitchen-sink Drama - a term used to describe modern plays exploring the domestic problems of ordinary people

Soliloquy - a type of monologue in which a character reveals their private thoughts directly to the audience

Stichomythia - choppy patterning of lines alternating between characters

Tragic Flaw - another term for hamartia

Tragi-comedy - plays which mix tragedy and comedy

General literary terminology

Allegory - a narrative with two meanings, an obvious surface one and a more subtle second meaning. For example, George Orwell's *Animal Farm* tells the story of animals rebelling against a tyrannical farmer. The animals' story is a political allegory about the rise of communism

Allusion - A reference to another work of literature. In *Frankenstein* Mary Shelley alludes to many other texts, most famously to *The Rime of the Ancient Mariner* and *Paradise Lost*

Antagonist - the main opponent of the central character. In *Othello*, Iago; in *Hamlet*, Claudius; in *Moby Dick*, the whale

Anti-hero - a protagonist with unheroic characteristics

Antithesis - is a rhetorical device containing opposites or, on a larger scale, the balancing of opposites in a stanza, speech or body of prose

Burlesque - a form of satire in which the style and content of a text is deliberately mismatched. For example, In Alexander Pope's *The Rape of the Lock*

Byronic Hero - a fascinating, moody Romantic figure, usually rebellious and solitary, often in sublime landscapes

Canon - a notional list of the great works of literature (often contested)

Characterisation - the methods used to create characters, such as visual description, interior monologue, through dialogue and so forth

Chiasmus - a figure of speech in which the word order of similar phrases is reversed. For example, in Yeats's 'An Irish Airman Foresees his Death': ' The years to come seemed waste of breath/ A waste of breath the years behind'

Collocation – patterns of words that often appear together, such as 'fish and chips'

Concrete - the opposite of abstract, referring to things not ideas.

Connotations - the implied meanings and associations of words

Dramatic Irony - when the audience know information of which the characters are unaware

Dsytopia - the opposite of Utopia; a world gone very wrong

Epiphany - a heightened moment of revelation

Epithet - an adjective or adjectival phrase that sticks like glue to a character. For example, *honest* Iago

Eponymous - named after the main character. For example, *Oliver Twist*.

Exposition - the setting of the scene and characters in a novel or play

Figurative language - metaphor, simile, symbol and personification

Foregrounding - bringing something to the reader's attention

Form - the shape, rather than the content, of a work of literature

Hyperbole - a synonym for exaggeration

Imagery - descriptive language that is either figurative or sensory (appeals to the senses)

In Media Res - a Latin term, meaning beginning in the middle of the story

Interior Monologue - the thoughts of a character

Intertextuality - the idea that all texts are connected to and composites of other texts

Juxtaposition - when contrasting ideas are placed together

Lexis - a synonym for vocabulary

Lexical Field - language associated with a particular activity, area or subject

Metalepsis - when the boundary between reality and fictional world is crossed. For example, if the author appears as a character in his or her own text.

Metonymy - where a concrete attribute of a thing stands in for it. For example, the crown for the monarchy

Mode - the style, manner or method with which the subject is treated

Monologue - a speech in the voice of a single character

Motif - a recurrent pattern of character, image, device, action or emotion in a work of literature

Naturalism - an extreme variant of realism tracing the effects of environments on characters

Onomatopoeia - Crash, bang, wallop

Parallelism - when similar sentences or phrases are side by side

Parody - an imitation that exaggerates or ridicules its original

Pastiche - an imitation of a text's style and concerns

Pastoral - presenting an idealised version of the countryside

Pathetic Fallacy - the use of nature to symbolise characters' feelings

Picaresque - a narrative that chronicles the misadventures of a likeable rogue

Plosive Alliteration - repetition of p,b, t and d sounds

Self-reflexivity - writing that draws attention to its own fictionality

Sibilance - the repetition of s sounds

Synaesthesia - the mixing of different senses. For example, in Seamus Heaney's poem 'Blackberry-picking' sound becomes physically tangible: *Bluebottles wove a strong gauze of sound*

Subtext - the meaning that lies beneath the surface of words

Symbol - a metaphor that has become universally decipherable. For instance, a dove symbolising peace or a rose love

Syntax - the order of words in a sentence

Vernacular - the ordinary language of a place or country

Zeugma – one word qualifying two others with different meanings: She broke his leg and his heart

24. Recommended Further Reading

Emagazine

The English Review

The Ode Less Travelled - Stephen Fry

The Art of Fiction - David Lodge

How to Analyse Poems: Art of Poetry - Neil Bowen, Matthew Curry, Michael Meally & Sally Rowley

Contemporary Poetry - Ian Brinton

52 Ways of Looking at a Poem - Ruth Padel

Beginning Theory, 3rd Edition - Peter Barry

How to Read a Poem - Terry Eagleton

The Edinburgh Introduction to Studying English Literature

Teaching English Literature 16-19 – Carol Atherton, Andrew Green & Gary Snapper

Writing Essays - Richard Marggraf Turley

About the authors

An experienced Head of English and freelance writer, **Neil Bowen** has been teaching English for nearly twenty years. He is the author many articles and resources for a range of publishers. Recently he worked on assignments for Poetry by Heart and currently has a series on teaching poetry in the pipeline with The Guardian. He is the creator and curator of the peripeteia project which aims to nurture high level literary discussion among students from different institutions. Neil has a Masters Degree in Literature and Education from Cambridge University and he is a member of Ofqual's experts panel for English. His literary interests include contemporary poetry and critical theory.

Michael Meally is an experienced teacher who is head of A-level English at Wells Cathedral School where he has taught for seven years. As well as degrees in Engineering and English Literature, Michael has an MA in American Literature and his literary interests are the short story, Greek tragedy, twentieth century literature, detective/crime fiction and postcolonial literature. He has written several articles for Emagazine as well as for our forthcoming *The Art of Analysing Poetry* series. Like Neil, Michael has a long track record of achieving outstanding examination results with his students at A-level.

With special thanks to our students Rebecca Toal and Judith Edmondson for kindly allowing us to use their essays; and also to Harry Coke for allowing us to use his illustration for *The Hairy Ape*.

CPSIA information can be obtained
at www.ICGtesting.com
Printed in the USA
LVOW01s1835250516

489941LV00009B/180/P

9 780993 077821